Software Project Management

Measures for Improving Performance

Software
Project
Management

Measures for Improving Performance

Robert Bruce Kelsey, Ph.D.

ſſſ
MANAGEMENTCONCEPTS

𝔪
MANAGEMENTCONCEPTS

8230 Leesburg Pike, Suite 800
Vienna, VA 22182
(703) 790-9595
Fax: (703) 790-1371
www.managementconcepts.com

Printed in the United States of America

Library of Congress Cataloging-in-Publication Data

Kelsey, Robert Bruce, 1954–
  Software project management : measures for improving performance / Robert Bruce Kelsey.
    p. cm.
  Includes bibliographical references and index.
  ISBN 1-56726-173-6 (pbk.)
    1. Computer software—Development—Management. I. Title.

QA76.76.D47K44 2006
005.1—dc22

                           2005054681

® *CMMI and Capability Maturity Model are registered in the U.S. Patent and Trademark Office by Carnegie Mellon University.*

SM *Personal Software Process and PSP are service marks of Carnegie Mellon University.*

TM *Rational Unified Process and RUP are registered trademarks of the Rational Software Corporation.*

About the Author

Robert Bruce Kelsey, Ph.D., is well recognized for his expertise in software engineering and project management. He has authored two dozen papers on software metrics, process improvement, and quality assurance. He is on the editorial or review boards of several industry journals and professional organizations, and as a member of the IEEE Standards Association he contributes to the IEEE learning technology and software standards. Also an experienced course developer and instructor with broad interests, Dr. Kelsey has taught in corporate, university, and community college settings on topics ranging from software quality assurance, to astronomy, to logic.

To Ted Davis

Table of Contents

Preface

If you've ever avoided checking your email for fear of finding another infestation of software bug reports from the test group, read this book. If you've ever wished you could identify problems with the development process *before* they turn into schedule disasters, this book will help you do that. If you're a software project manager in a low-maturity organization where you have no Software Engineering Process Group and no Project Management Office (PMO), or you're trying to use your influence as a project manager to drive some department-wide process improvement, read on.

Software Project Management: Measures for Improving Performance is about using software measures to identify and mitigate the software development project risks that are typically associated with development process inefficiencies and product quality problems. This is not a tutorial in statistical process control, nor is it a handbook for PMOs setting up portfolio reporting and control procedures. The focus here is on analyzing and overcoming day-to-day crises that keep software project managers busy in between project status reporting periods.

● HOW ARE WE DOING? *NOT* HOW DID WE DO?

This book is intended for software project managers and development staff who want to use software measurement as a "real-time" performance indicator. The measures presented here will help you answer questions such as:

- Are we on track, and if not, can we get back on track?
- Are the effort estimates accurate? If not, how inaccurate are they?
- Are the estimates accurate but the workload greater than expected?
- How can we plan, in advance, the effort required to fix defects when we don't know how many there will be or when they will appear?
- Can the data coming from the test group help us estimate more accurately when we'll be finished?

This book presents a "bottom-up" approach to software measurement. It identifies the key measures and shows you what they can (and cannot) tell you about the status of your product and schedule. It focuses on interpreting data to avoid surprises, not on process control. I don't talk about statistical process control because I'm assuming that most readers won't have any defined and consistently followed processes. Nor is there anything about creating metrics dashboards or scorecards, because I'm assuming that no one in your boardroom cares.

Yet.

And that's an important qualifier. Software project managers and their harried development teams often have to be change agents in an environment that sees no need for change, only more effort. But quantitative data on software products and project performance, however rudimentary or imprecise, is the Archimedes lever that can move the earth. What you learn here will help you convince the rest of the business that quantitative software management really can improve the bottom line.

The chapters that follow will show you how to design and position a measurement effort in the business as a whole, what measures you should implement, how to interpret the results of your measurements, and how to apply that knowledge to solve some typical challenges in software development. With a problem-tracking system and the help of your team, you can collect, analyze, and apply all these measures with relatively little effort, in a relatively short time, and without any tools other than a spreadsheet program.

● WHAT WILL I LEARN?

The focus of *Software Project Management: Measures for Improving Performance* is on using measurement to improve day-to-day performance in your software projects. You will learn how measurement programs should be put together, how the measures interrelate, and how they can be used to support one another. You will learn what to measure, when to measure it, and, most important, how to interpret the data you collect so you can diagnose and correct problems in both product quality and team productivity.

The book takes you from simple run rate data through to more advanced measures such as phase containment and cost of poor quality. Along the way, you'll find many examples of how to combine measures to solve complex problems such as defective components, schedule-slip recovery, and estimation accuracy.

Many of the chapters end with exercises to help you apply the concepts presented. Work through them; don't skip them! If you apply what you've learned as you go through this book, you should be able to start setting up your measurement effort long before you turn the last page.

● CAN I APPLY THIS INFORMATION IMMEDIATELY?

The tools and techniques discussed here can be applied even in the most rudimentary development environments. You don't need a rack of servers loaded with expensive CASE tools or financial and productivity management application packages. You don't need to wait until you hire on with a CMMI® level 3 organization. All you need to get started is a spreadsheet application and time and defect data. Successful use of software measurement data depends on how effectively you think about the data you have, not on the technology you used to obtain that data.

● DO I NEED TO BE A SOFTWARE DEVELOPER TO UNDERSTAND THIS MATERIAL?

Obviously, the more you know about software development, the better you will be at managing development projects. You don't have to be an expert in software architecture, design, development, and validation to apply these measures, however. You only have to be a facilitator.

There's no reason why you can't involve your project team in architecting and implementing your measures. In fact, there's one very good reason to do so: ownership. Development teams are more likely to see the value in measurement if they have had input into the measures and how they are going to be used. Draw on their expertise and experience when identifying causes for run-rate variances. Have them determine the best measurement points for defect injection phase measures, or the categories for time and effort measures.

A few team brainstorming sessions early in the project will not only help you identify and specify your measures, but will serve as good team-building exercises as well. Laying out the workflow on a whiteboard as a team exercise is a good place to start. You might be surprised to find how little one group knows about another group's responsibilities or about how their group's activities impact other groups. After that, work through some of the exercises with your project team (particularly those at the end of Chapters 1, 2, and 4). These can be very helpful in coaxing implementation details out of your project team.

● CAN I USE THIS TEXT IN MY COURSE OR SEMINAR?

This book is an ideal core text for seminars and short courses on topics such as improving software project performance, project-level software measurements, and measurement data analysis. It can also be used as a supplemental text in courses and seminars covering the discipline of software project management. The *Instructor's Guide*, available separately from the publisher (pubsupport@management concepts.com), explains the key concepts in each chapter and provides discussion points for getting students involved in thinking about and applying the material presented in each chapter.

● THE GAME'S AFOOT

My first exposure to project management methods came many years ago when, as a software development lead, I took a seminar in software project management. I knew there had to be some way to improve how my team got its work done, but I wasn't convinced that what we did warranted the honorific title of "project," and I had my doubts about the "management" part.

The instructor started off the seminar with two remarks that immediately put me at ease. First, he said we should consider everything we do as a project. Whether we are developing software, moving to a new apartment, or building a space station, we need to plan, observe, and react. Then, he presented two analogies to project management. One was the symphony conductor, who merely coordinated the activities of the musical experts in the concert hall. That model, he warned us, simply didn't work in the software industry.

Instead, he suggested Sir Arthur Conan Doyle's famous character Sherlock Holmes as the exemplar. Always looking for clues, always thinking ahead and balancing multiple possible outcomes, ever ready to react to his opponent's movements, Doyle's detective displayed all the analytical skills, imagination, and ingenuity that software project managers need to succeed. We could also learn something from his "style," the instructor suggested: Holmes "managed" nothing, but he also never lost control.

In that same spirit, I hope you will find this book indispensable as you match wits with that mysterious and elusive opponent, "successful software development."

Bruce Kelsey
South Amana, Iowa

Acknowledgments

The author thanks Thomas Miller of T. R. Miller and Associates for his support along the way and Ralph Williams of Cooliemon, LLC, for the initial impetus for this project. Thanks are due as well to Sheila Kelsey, who edited the entire manuscript and patiently removed the same peculiarities of style she removed from my other two books.

CHAPTER

1

Measures, Goals, and Strategies

Some of us climb mountains because they're there. Some of us read books to know we are not alone. Some of us measure software just so we and our teams can survive the project, and some of us measure software to ascertain whether the development processes are in control.

■ MEASURING PERFORMANCE WITHIN A PROJECT

There's a big difference between measuring the performance *of* a software development project and measuring performance *within* a software development project. Software project performance is typically measured in high-maturity organizations. In these organizations, the business processes are documented and audited for efficiency. The development organization has corporate support and funding for formal software quality assurance and process improvement. In high-maturity organizations, the software project as a whole is measured as if it were a complete business process in itself: it's effective (delivers on time), it's efficient (meets budget), and it's profitable (results in margin or profit).

In such organizations, metrics programs are a tool for measuring project capability and compliance. The paradigms for such software metrics programs are the well-established CMMI® level 4 organizations with fully functional organizational process performance and quantitative project management in place. With their substantial historical data and standardized and audited processes, these organizations can make statistically valid inferences from their measures about the project as a whole, identifying deviations and diagnosing process failures.

Much has been written about these formal software metrics programs. Any organization that wants to start an organization-wide, executive-sponsored software metrics program can follow the IEEE standards or the CMMI® model. When it comes to implementation details, dozens of books explain how to integrate measurement across the entire product and project lifecycle or how to use the data to improve your organization. When you need more extensive advice, read the classic texts by Grady, Fenton, Myers, Kan, and others (see Further Reading). They'll tell you what worked for Hewlett-Packard, the National Aeronautics and Space Administration, and a host of other companies with ample revenue streams and a senior management staff committed to product quality.

The problem is that many software practitioners don't work for mature, or even maturing, software companies. Some work in situations where the software development organization is one of those "challenged cost centers"—costs too much and needs attention—but none of the executives knows what to do about it. There's no enlightened senior management to endorse software process improvement initiatives, nor any highly respected and well compensated consultants to guide the program when senior management interest falters because the results are too slow in coming. There's no Software Quality Assurance or Software Engineering Process Group to bear the brunt of the work of process improvement.

Some software practitioners work in dot-coms or MIS/IT shops, suffocating under the pressure to deliver on impossible schedules without requirements, designs, or even adequate resources. There's simply no room for documented processes when there are four de-

velopers in a one-person cubicle. There's no time for reviews or au-
dits when just getting the code done will take 12 hours a day, every
day, for the next 18 weeks.

You can't worry about maturity levels when you're always living on the edge. Project managers, development and test managers,
and team leads in situations like these have to find a way around the
crisis of the hour. They need software measurement data that they
can use in the day-to-day decisions, not in the next quarterly business review. They need to measure their performance against the
project schedule, not the project's compliance with historical norms
for Estimate at Completion.

Measuring progress entails far more than checking off a line
item in the work breakdown structure. Projects need to be viewed as
organisms rather than task lists. In the human body, different types
of cells perform different tasks, in different locations and at different
times. In projects, different people in different roles work individually to complete tasks that in turn trigger other people to begin or
complete their tasks. You can't diagnose and treat a disease in an
organism unless you know all the symptoms and how they interact.
Similarly, you can't diagnose and treat performance problems in a
project unless you know what symptoms to look for, where to look
for them, and what to do about them.

● TWO WAYS TO USE MEASUREMENT

Some people use software measurement like they use a daily
weather forecast. They want to know how to prepare for the day, so
an overview is all they need. Knowing the estimated average temperature and whether it will be rainy or sunny, they can make decisions about how to dress for the day and whether they should try to
run an errand over lunch. Similarly, from a few department-wide indicators, the Director of Software Development can tell whether her
projects will complete successfully or whether she should contact a
headhunter on her lunch break.

For this class of measurement users, the details aren't particularly important. They know that it will be hotter on the streets

downtown than it will be in the shaded streets of the suburbs. The temperature isn't likely to fluctuate far from the forecast. Of course, there's always the chance that even a sunny day will suddenly turn nasty if certain conditions develop. If the forecast doesn't show that as a possibility, they're content to leave the umbrella behind. Similarly, since the earned value across the projects is tracking close to expectations, our Director of Software Development can go out for lunch and not worry about whether the VP will be waiting in her office when she returns.

Others use software measurement as some kind of archeological dig. They examine papyri bearing curious line glyphs and tablets with weather-worn bar carvings, from which they draw lessons from the past. For these folks, measurements are useful because they reveal how people and processes and projects really work. Measures tell stories about how teams succeeded or why they failed. What was life like on the streets of Cubicle City when the earthquake struck, the build crumbled, and the Atlantis Project slid beneath the waves of the Sea of Red Ink?

For this class of measurement users, the details are extremely important. They know that software development projects succeed or fail requirement by requirement, code line by code line, defect report by defect report. Trend lines are all well and good so long as the environmental factors don't change. If any of them do change, the forecast can become invalid, with a sunny morning quickly turning into a dreadful afternoon. This class of measurement users knows that if you have detailed measurement data that shows how different types of events affect people, products, and schedules, then you can improve the durability and reliability of your forecasts and plans.

These two perspectives are not incompatible. In fact, both are necessary for a successful measurement program. Unless senior management can derive some operational and strategic benefit from the indicators you put on their Quarterly Business Review Dashboard, they aren't likely to give your efforts much financial or logistical support. On the other hand, unless you've demonstrated that you can manage the chaos of your day-to-day tasks, you won't be around to see them write the check.

Nevertheless, that's no excuse to start counting everything in sight. Improperly conceived, a measurement effort can turn into an expensive exercise in arithmetic that causes more problems than it solves. Development teams wouldn't think of starting to code without first doing some kind of design work. A measurement effort deserves the same care and preparation.

● WHAT IS SOFTWARE MEASUREMENT?

Put aside for a moment everything you know about software. Forget what you learned from Pressman and Kan. Ignore what the tools vendors have told you. With your slate clean, answer the following deceptively simple question: What are we measuring when we measure software, and why do we measure it?

On the face of it, the answer seems straightforward. We are measuring a process—the tasks involved in developing software. We are also measuring a thing—the software product's functional "content" and its conformance with specifications and quality requirements. This answer, however, merely identifies the two major domains of inquiry process and product. It tells us the areas we want to measure, but it doesn't help us decide what exactly we want to measure, why we want to measure that instead of something else, or what we ought to do with the data once we have it.

Those two domains of inquiry are huge, and they span a host of interrelated components. So, there won't be a simple answer to the question. When we investigate "software," we are examining design and development processes, validation processes, customer needs and savvy at various times, code, documents, specifications, online help, etc., etc. To make matters more interesting, very few of these components are actually tangible things.

For example, requirements drift is not a thing in itself—it's a change, a delta. For convenience sake, we like to locate drift in the physical difference between a requirements document at time A and time B. That lexical difference isn't the shift itself, however. It's the symptom or the trace of the measurement target, which is the event of drift. And that event is very hard to analyze effectively. It might be that the customer simply changed its collective mind. It might be that the systems engineers neglected to probe customer requirements deeply enough to determine the real requirements. It might be that the requirements never really changed, but were just inaccurately documented or inappropriately interpreted during the development cycle.

Similarly, we often speak of the source code as the end product of software development. Source code isn't a product in the typical sense of the term, and its transference to a CD isn't the end result of the process. The source code is a code: like any language, it is the result of experience and thinking and analyzing and communicating. Like any language, it only exists as a language when it is used or executed. The process isn't complete even when the software is first used by the customer's employees to successfully accomplish some task. It's an ongoing process with many exit points and many decision milestones. Between the time the request for proposal arrives and the time the customer signs an end-of-warranty agreement, hundreds of factors are involved in specifying, designing, creating, testing, producing, distributing, using, and evaluating "software."

If "software" is really a collection of multiple attributes evaluated by many people over a long period of time, just what are we supposed to measure? The simple answer is: We measure what will help us get our work done.

All measurement has a rationale, a purpose. It has an audience. It is a means to an end. Someone is going to use the data for some purpose. They will draw conclusions from it. They may change project plans or scope or cost estimates based on those conclusions. Those actions will in turn affect other aspects of the project, maybe even the business itself.

● WHAT DO YOU WANT TO ACCOMPLISH WITH MEASUREMENT?

Since all measurement has a purpose, you should start off by deciding what you want to accomplish through measurement:

➠ Do you want to show that your project team really is working at over 100 percent capacity?

➠ Do you want to prove that the product is a quality product, maybe even of higher quality than might be expected given the lack of support you get from senior management and sales?

➠ Do you want to use the data to help change the workload of some of your staff?

➠ Do you want to be able (in some loose sense) to predict whether changes will cause more risk, effort, or cost?

Most likely, you are turning to measurement to help you do one or more of the following:

• Understand what is affecting your current performance.
• Baseline your performance.
• Address deficiencies and get better at what you do.
• Manage risks associated with changes in schedules, requirements, personnel allocations, etc.
• Improve your estimation capabilities.

The one aspect that's missing from this list and the one you would do well not to forget is bringing visibility to your area. Business executives too often treat software development as a black-box component in their organization. They forget to give it the same attention they give more typical segments of operations like manufacturing, packaging, and shipping. Software development organizations are so used to being treated like some third-party order fulfillment service that they forget that their departments need the same level of attention and involvement from senior management that the operations departments enjoy.

As a result, your measures should help you address both the financial and the political aspects of software development. You'll need the usual bottom-line measures such as "on time" and "at spec." But you'll also want to call attention to the operation of the department within the organization as a whole, showing it as a consumer of the work of some business units upstream in the total workflow, and as a supplier to other business units downstream in that workflow.

Of course, we don't want our measures to be just demarcations, lines on some corporate ruler used to see if we measure up to the CFO's or COO's expectations. We also want our measures to be feedback loops. When we do measure up, we want our measurements to show us what we did right. When we don't meet expectations, we want our measurements to show us why and where we fell short and what to do about it next time.

● A COMMITMENT TO THE FUTURE

There's an even more significant implication for software project management here. Software measurement is not just a tool—it's a commitment. Measures aren't tossed away at the end of the project with all the network diagrams and resource graphs that have cluttered up your desk for several months. The measurement data holds keys to your future success.

Looked at day to day, every project seems different. The schedule, the deliverables, the customers, the budget, and the resources aren't quite the same as they were on the last project. There are new challenges, new obstacles to overcome. Yet, in every project there's the need to know exactly where you are in the project, how much it cost to get you to where you are today, and how likely it is that you will complete the project on time and on budget.

This is where software measurement becomes a commitment. Put in place the measures you need to be successful, not just in today's project but in next year's projects. Don't assume that software metrics is something a development manager or a Software Engineering Process Group is supposed to do. If there's no measurement program, implement one. It's in everyone's best interest, most of all yours!

● THINK GLOBALLY, ACT LOCALLY

It takes a long time to move organizations up the maturity ladder or to get them fully functional as ISO 9001 companies. The entire organization has to change the way it works, and organizations move slowly. If you work in a company that is not interested in IEEE 12207 or CMMI®, there are limits to what you will initially be able to accomplish. For example, many high-maturity, program-level measures require coordinating data across departments, and it is unlikely that you will be able to get this data early in your efforts.

Nonetheless, you should approach your software measurement effort as if it were a company-wide effort. You are obviously the first and most important user of your measures, and your choice of measures and measurement points should improve your chances of success. But your success will be just the beginning. Your peer project managers will want to adopt your best practices. Senior management will want to see more of the quantitative data you are using to manage your project in real time. What starts out as a means to get you through the project might well blossom into a company-wide effort. So plan accordingly:

1. Architect the effort, establishing measurement hierarchies and interdependencies. (Chapter 2 will take you through one such architecture.)
2. Design the effort, so you know why and when you want to collect data. (Chapters 3 and 4 will describe the measures, how they interrelate, and when to collect them.)
3. Use the measures. (Chapters 4 through 6 will guide you through interpreting and displaying the data, and Chapter 6 will offer several examples of using measurement information to solve typical development project problems.)

● IDENTIFY AREAS OF OPPORTUNITY

Throughout this book, we'll focus on getting you the information you need to manage the project's workload. By workload, I don't mean just producing code or completing test cases. That's only the visible, explicitly valued aspect of most workdays. Certainly, a project manager wants to know how well his or her group is performing at the level of the work breakdown structure item. On a day-to-day basis, though, the project manager also needs to have data that he or she can use to make and to justify decisions, to plan and to estimate, and so forth. This data is just as important as productivity or defect density. In practical terms, this means that you also need to take into consideration all the planning, reviewing, bickering, and rework that so quickly fill up the empty slots on everyone's daily calendar.

When starting up a measurement effort, identify those areas that cause the most surprises and decide how to monitor them. Answering the following questions will typically uncover areas of opportunity for measurement and improvement:

- ➡ Are the requirements always changing?
- ➡ Does it take longer than expected to finalize the requirements?
- ➡ Does the development team make changes to the requirements and/or design documents right up to the last minute?
- ➡ Does coding take longer than estimated?
- ➡ Does the development team have to add code tasks to the project plan in the middle of the development phase?
- ➡ Does the transition to testing often uncover problems with planned tasks or estimates?
- ➡ Is the test phase always full of unwelcome surprises that force schedule slips?
- ➡ Is internal documentation delivered on time, and is it accurate?
- ➡ Is external documentation delivered on time, and is it accurate?

As you consider what needs to be improved in these areas, set your sights on changes you can make within the boundaries of your own group. Focus on things you can control—areas where you'd like to be better prepared, more efficient, or more disciplined—and start there.

● SELECT AN OPERATIONAL MEASURE AND STRATEGY

The four key operational measures—defects, time, cost, and risk—will provide you ample information for managing and improving your current situation. The measures are interrelated, and it is helpful to select a primary strategy for setting up your measurement effort. Since many project risks and costs are directly affected by variance in defects and time, the choice of strategy is really between product quality and productivity.

Defects take time to fix. Unplanned time quickly turns into schedule risks. Schedule risks can become increased project costs. So if your defect rates are high, focus your attention on defect-related measurements.

If your defect rates are not high, but your estimates are generally off, then time would be the best measure to start with. Inaccurate estimates of time increase risk to meeting milestones, which in turn can become additional costs. Moreover, developers and testers working under pressure can make mistakes, which increases product quality risks.

Some of the reasons for inaccurate estimates or plans may be out of your control. Likewise, some of the root causes for defects may fall within departments other than your own. Nonetheless, measuring time or defects will give you enough information about your own organization to improve your performance and lower your risks.

● A STRATEGY FOR ADDRESSING PRODUCT QUALITY

Suppose you decide to start your measurement effort by measuring defects because there are a lot of them and they take time that's not included in the project plan. This is really two issues: (1) defect rates, and (2) estimating the effort required to correct defects. Better information related to the first issue will help resolve the second issue, so focus first on defects rather than estimates of time to fix.

Before you can glean any useful information from defect rates, you have to know what kinds of defects affect your projects. Ask yourself the following questions:

➡ Do you know where defects are introduced in the development process?
➡ Do you know where most of your defects are first discovered?

➡ What kinds of defects occur (e.g., functional, usability, data integrity)?

➡ What kind of defect appears most often?

➡ How do you decide whether a defect has to be fixed right away or not?

➡ If your bug tracking system categorizes defects by severity and priority, are those categories really helpful in determining the nature of the defect and its impact both on the release and on the customer?

➡ What kind of testing generates the most defects?

➡ Is this testing related to validating customer requirements or to proving the product works on specific environments, or is it another kind of testing?

You probably won't have answers to all these questions immediately. In fact, you may have to use the measurement effort to provide you with some of the answers. The point to remember is that defects don't just happen; they are caused. Once you know the conditions under which they appear, you can start managing the project environment to limit their effect on the project.

Using your answers to the questions above, set up a defect profile:

1. Identify the characteristics of the defects.
2. Group the defects according to some classification scheme.
3. Identify the root cause(s) for each class of defect.
4. Determine if different classes of defect typically have different impacts on the project and the customer.

Now that you have the profile, you can look for appropriate measurement points:

5. Identify the typical project milestones or phases of development and test efforts.
6. Make a list of the questions you would like answered at these measurement points. Don't worry about the data itself yet. The goal of this step is to identify as best you can the information you want to extract from the data.

Once you have set up your problem tracking system (discussed in detail in Chapter 4), this approach is fairly easy to implement. It will give you some insight into where your own activities may be producing defects or not catching them. It will also give you visibility into where other organizations may be contributing to the defect rate. Only indirectly will it improve your productivity or streamline your workflow, because it is focused on obstacles rather than opportunities for efficiency. For that information, you'll need to implement another kind of strategy.

● A STRATEGY FOR ADDRESSING PRODUCTIVITY AND WORKFLOW

The observed defect rate is low in many development environments. What gets the most visibility are schedule overruns and resource cost overruns. In this situation, your measures need to focus on how the developers and testers get their work done: where the process is efficient and where it is inefficient. Just as the defect strategy began with a profile, the productivity strategy needs to begin with a profile. In this case, you want to know what "effective use of time" means in your organization, and how that currently maps to your project plans and work breakdown structures.

The first step is to recognize where your organization's primary focus lies. Ask yourself the following questions:

➡ *Is your corporate climate laissez-faire as long as the dates are met?* If your team is left pretty much alone so it can try to meet impossible deadlines, then you'll want to focus on the actual time to complete tasks. This will give you quantitative support when you escalate problems or when your management makes unrealistic commitments on your behalf. It will also allow you to plan more accurately for, and manage risks related to, the commitments you currently have.

➡ *Alternatively, does your corporate environment revere billable hours?* If so, do you need to demonstrate that your resources are fully utilized on their assigned projects?

➡ *Do you also need to know how much time is spent doing other tasks that are mission-critical to some stakeholders in your*

project but are not critical to your project per se? If your resources are "publicly" allocated to your project, while in reality they are often pulled off to help someone else, you may
want to track time misspent on interruptions as well as direct
labor hours.

➡ *What level of granularity is required to meet the organization's
expectations?*

➡ *What level of granularity do* you *think you need as a project
manager?*

➡ *Do you need to track time by resource and by task, or just by
total charged hours and time period (say, all hours charged to
the project by all team members for the previous week)?*

➡ *Do you need to track time to a line item on a work breakdown
structure, or to the various development activities that contribute to that task?*

Once you've decided whether your goal is to measure time
spent, time misspent, or both, and once you've decided what level
of granularity is required, you can look for appropriate measurement
points:

1. Categorize the project tasks into types of activities and/or
into phases of project activity.
2. Identify the significant obstacles or interruptions that your
project team will face.
3. Using any existing data you may have and interviews with
the project team members, establish the duration range (the
anticipated minimum and maximum) for the categories of
tasks and the obstacles or interruptions.
4. Make a list of the questions you would like answered at these
measurement points. Different tasks will probably prompt
different questions, as will different kinds of obstacles. Don't
worry about the data itself yet; the goal of this step is to
identify as best you can the information you want to extract
from the data.

A time-focused approach will give you some insight into where
you can streamline your own activities. It will also give you visibility

into time constraints or time conflicts within your project team. The information garnered from the analysis phase can be turned around immediately into better planning for the next development cycle in the current project.

● APPLYING WHAT YOU'VE LEARNED

The following exercises will help you position and define your measurement effort within the rest of the organization.

Exercise 1-1: A Clear Rationale

1. What does your company value (innovation, revenue, quality, professional development, etc.)?
2. What are your department's specific business goals? If your department doesn't have any explicit business goals, what goals do you think it should have?
3. Why do you want to measure your processes and products? Phrase your answer so it addresses both the values and goals.

Exercise 1-2: A Strategy to Meet Real Needs

1. If you could change three aspects of your own work environment, what would you change?
2. If you could change three aspects of your team's or department's work environment, what would you change?
3. What processes in the organization have an impact on these six aspects? (The processes don't have to be documented, formal processes; they could be just "how things get done around here" or, even more informally, patterns of behavior.)
4. Rank the six aspects from highest to lowest priority.
5. What should you measure to leverage change in these six areas? How can these measures help improve the processes or behaviors that affect these six areas?
6. As you think about what you would like to change in the way you manage projects, think also about how this change

can be motivated and who owns making the actual change. For example, if you need to motivate people to implement a new process, you may have to focus first on what the lack of a process costs and only later on how well people are performing the process.

Implementing a Measurement Architecture

"My project kickoff meeting is two days away. Why should I take the time to figure out a measurement architecture?"

That's a perfectly legitimate question, for which there are two very practical answers:

1. You will not have time in the project to come up with new measures when the ones you hastily implement next week don't give you the information you need.
2. If the data you collect misleads you into incorrect diagnoses and corrective actions, you will not have time in the project for mid-course corrections.

Software project management is such a challenging career because it involves so much more than mere coordination and logistics. Software requirements are never as precise as building codes. Software designs are never as detailed as blueprints. Developers and testers have their own unique ways of doing things; even if they are certified in their fields, they will not perform with the same consistency and predictability you can expect of other skilled professionals in, say, electrical or mechanical engineering.

When you oversee a construction project, the main challenge is getting the pieces together on time and putting them together in the right sequence. When you manage a software project, the main challenge is getting the people and the information to fit together. Even well-written requirements can be interpreted differently. The best design spec in the world still doesn't tell the developer exactly how to structure the line-by-line logic in the code. Measuring software development isn't as simple as measuring tolerances and lengths. In a software project, progress (or lack of progress) isn't always visible.

You don't need a master's degree in statistics to implement a software measurement architecture. All you need is to know what obstacles you will face in the project and what data you will need to overcome those obstacles. This chapter will help you work out the details for yourself.

● MEASURES ARE ANSWERS TO QUESTIONS

It's important to distinguish between a measurement and the significance of that measurement. A measure is simply a value for a variable, a notch on some scale. Inches and yards are simply points on the scale of length. Centiliters and grams are milestones of volume and weight. We seldom take measurements for their own sake. We usually measure something so we can answer a question or solve a problem. For example:

➡ Is the software ready to ship?
- We measure the defect rate to determine if it is dropping. We measure the number of tests completed to ensure that we are completing our tasks.

➡ Will the project complete on time?
- We determine how much work is left to do by examining the task completion percentages. We chart our resource utilization to determine if we have assigned a reasonable or unreasonable workload.

➡ Was the project a good return on investment?
- We compute the actual direct labor costs for project tasks compared to the estimates to determine resource-related project performance. We measure customer satisfaction or

defects after sale or follow-on sales to determine if the project improved perceived quality, reduced warranty costs, or indirectly increased income.

Whatever measures we choose, they are just raw data until they are manipulated and interpreted. So the challenge for any measurement architecture is to establish not only what measurements are to be made but also how those measures are to be interpreted.

● THE ISO/IEC 15939 ARCHITECTURE

The architecture used here is based on the ISO/IEC 15939:2002 standard *Software engineering – Software measurement process*. It's not the only architecture you could use, but it has three advantages:

1. It is an international standard and will lend credibility and portability to your measurement effort for both on-shore and off-shore projects.
2. It emphasizes the why of measurement, not just the what.
3. Its architecture is compatible with other software models such as CMMI® or RUP®.

In the ISO/IEC model, the process begins with the establishment of "information needs" rather than with an inventory of what data is currently available or easily obtained. The rationale for this is very simple: whatever data you collect has to be presented to its user community in a way that they can understand. It has to be useful to them; that is, it has to answer their particular questions or solve their particular problems.

That standard also identifies several key aspects of measurement programs:

- Measurable concepts
- Base measures
- Derived measures
- Models and indicators.

Measurable Concepts

Measurable concepts point out how different measures are interrelated. For example, a typical measurable concept in project management is "project labor costs." A typical model for that measure specifies that "cost" will be measured using resource effort in person hours and a standard transfer cost from the cost centers of the business to the profit centers of the business. The person hours are a base measure and their transposition into cost is a derived measure.

A model may support several indicators, each of which identifies some aspect of the model. In the case of the "project labor costs" model, the related indicators include the average cost per developer, the cost per developed component, etc. Just as units of measurement must be interpreted, these indicators must be evaluated according to decision criteria to determine if the product or process is within tolerable levels or if some corrective action is necessary.

The ISO/IEC standard's terminology may seem a bit cumbersome, especially to those whose introduction to software metrics started with counting defects or lines of code. One of the standard's goals is to help users architect a measurement program, not just start collecting data haphazardly. The architectural aspect is important because measurement is not standardized across the software industry. The industry is generally in agreement about what measurable concepts are important, but there's less consensus on the models, indicators, and criteria.

Consider the measurable concept of developer productivity. Many a project or engineering manager has tried to measure developer productivity by direct labor hours on a component, only to find that the COO expected productivity to be measured in lines of code per day. "After all," the manager is told, "if companies can measure the productivity of manufacturing line personnel by the number of units they complete per day, why can't we measure a software developer's productivity by the number of lines of code he or she produces each day?"

Anyone familiar with the hour-by-hour tasks of a software developer will recognize that the COO's model is seriously flawed. First, it assumes that lines of code are the only work product produced. Second, it neglects all the other tasks that a developer accomplishes in a day that can be considered part of the developer's productive output. The model's prime indicator—lines of code per developer per day—may well be a measurable entity but it won't support legitimate conclusions about productivity. The underlying model simply isn't a realistic model of what developers do.

The point to remember is that any architectural effort must begin by identifying the information needs of the whole organization, not just your own needs. These needs will usually differ in their level of abstraction, so you should anticipate having to create a hierarchy of indicators. To a test manager, the number of defects discovered per test run may be a critical indicator of product quality. To a quality manager familiar with industry standards, defect density might be more important. To the COO, cost of maintenance across multiple releases is probably a more interesting indicator.

With the larger picture of information needs in mind, you can then determine which base measures you will need, which derived measures you will need, and which models you will use to roll up all this data into indicators and sound bites for the user community. The relationship between these items is illustrated in Figure 2-1.

Base Measures

Base measures are the simplest and thus the "lowest" item in the measurement hierarchy. These are measures of a single attribute of a product or a process, such as lines of code per component, defects found in testing, or time charged to a project task. Ideally, the attribute will have only one cause, source, or contributing factor. Thus, time charged to a project task is a better base measure than total time charged to a project, simply because the total project time includes many more factors (i.e., many more variables) than the time charged to a single task.

Keep in mind that conclusions drawn from measurement of a single factor attribute are more cogent than conclusions drawn from measurement of an attribute with multiple contributing factors. With multi-factor attributes, there's no way to tell which variables actually affected the measurement. As a result, comparing measurements made at different times can lead to false diagnoses and conclusions.

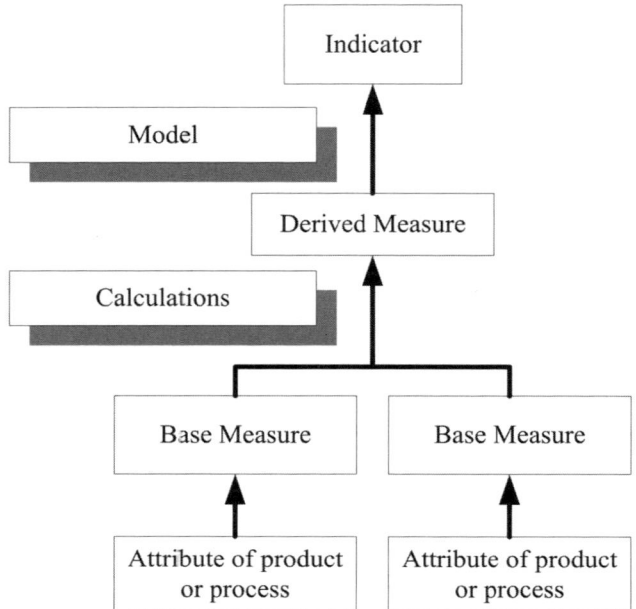

Figure 2-1 ● ISO/IEC 15939:2002 Measurement Architecture

For example, suppose we compare "total charged time" for four different projects. What can we legitimately conclude from that data *alone*? Nothing, except that the total charged times differ. We can glean no information about the productivity of the developers, the difficulty of the tasks involved, the quality of what was produced, etc. We can't see through the data points to whatever is contributing to the difference.

Some base measures in software development are neither quantitative nor single-factor. For example, the rating schemes used for "severity" and "priority" in many problem report systems are used as base measures by both the engineering and the quality functions, but the attribute being measured really is a collection of attributes. If it is impossible to separate out all other related attributes, then the measure should be constrained in such a way as to render all those other factors irrelevant. That way the data is consistent, even though what's actually being measured is multifaceted.

For example, the "severity" of a particular software failure is a subjective determination made by the customer or the support person handling the trouble call. The degree of subjectivity is constrained in the reporting tool by the use of a pull-down list of possible values—critical, high, and medium, for example. The interpretation of the values is standardized to the extent possible by training employees in what the values mean, when to apply them, and how to interpret them.

Derived Measures

Derived measures are the result of combining two or more base measures. When we compute the increase of lines of code per component across two releases, we are creating a derived measure from two distinct measurements of the component's lines of code. When we graph earned value, we are creating a measure derived from planned effort (or cost) and actual effort (or cost).

Since indicators are derived from a collection of other measures, they too can be considered a type of derived measure. The distinction between derived measures and indicators seems especially blurry when the indicator is derived directly from base measures. The distinction lies in use rather than calculation:

➡ Derived measures are interim steps in interpreting the state of products and processes.
➡ Indicators are the conceptual flags that signal a healthy or unhealthy state.

For example, the industry standard indicator of defect density is computed from the value of "defects recorded per time period X" and the value of "lines of code at the end of time period X." In this case, we have combined base measures of incidence and time to get two new values that are then combined again to get the indicator. The same is true of the other derived measures illustrated in Figure 2-2. Requirements changes and time are combined into requirements stability. Baseline project plan tasks and duration are combined with the actual time expended to determine percent complete.

Base Measure	Derived Measure	Model	Indicator
Time per project task	Percent complete	Total task percent complete expressed as total of project budgeted cost of work performed	Earned Value
Number of defects reported	Defects reported per project phase	Defects reported per project phase expressed as percent of total number of known defects	Phase Containment

Figure 2-2 ■ Relationship between Base Measures, Derived Measures, Models, and Indicators

Models and Indicators

Models are the calculations used to turn base or derived measures into indicators. They are called models because the calculations assume that there are some significant relationships between measures and attributes. These relationships may be causal or quasi-causal, as when an increase in the number of requirements changes usually results in additional cost later in the project. These relationships may also be simply conceptually useful, as in the case where one measure helps us interpret another.

We encountered an example of the conceptual relationship between measures when we briefly looked at total charged time for a project. Total charged time is a multifaceted attribute and is thus hard to interpret. As we saw, one would normally have to apply other measures such as developer productivity, task difficulty, and product quality to help understand the situation. In planning a measurement effort, you should recognize the limitations of your models and plan for any supplemental derived measures that might be helpful.

It is very important to understand the assumptions on which your models are based. Take, for example, the indicator "earned value." Earned value is an excellent example of the difference between measuring the performance of a project as a whole and measuring performance within a project. The project-level measurement of earned value assumes that the only relevant attributes are project tasks, planned and actual effort, and associated costs. The model ignores factors that might affect the effort, such as cultural, social, and psychological effects on the project team's performance.

Project-level earned value also assumes that "effort" is properly measured by time and cost. Earned value itself doesn't take into account developer skill level, task complexity, etc. Properly done, estimations will accommodate those factors. But the indicator itself contains no correction in its model if the estimations are inaccurate or didn't take into account factors such as skill levels and complexity.

Finally, earned value assumes that project task completion can be legitimately modeled at a high level of abstraction as a linear series of events. This usually reasonable assumption can get you into trouble when the project involves formal iterative development methods or when the requirements management processes are weak. In either of these cases, design tasks (as well as code development and validation) are often interpretive, cyclic, and, in the worst case, unpredictable in terms of duration and resource allocations.

In Chapter 5 we'll look at another use of earned value that focuses on the day-to-day activities of the project team. This view of performance within the project gets into the hour-by-hour details of the staff. While some of the data coming out of this approach to earned value can be used in calculating the project-level earned value, the primary goal of this approach is to get resource-specific performance data and use it for risk management and for future estimations. For the moment, it's sufficient to point out that this approach is a cornerstone of the highly acclaimed Personal Software Process[SM], which tackles typical project risks from the bottom up, cubicle by cubicle, rather than top down from the project plan.

● PUTTING THE ARCHITECTURE TO WORK

When properly architected, a measurement effort can give you essential information about your products and processes with only a handful of base and derived measures. Figure 2-3 shows the building blocks for defect density and earned value.

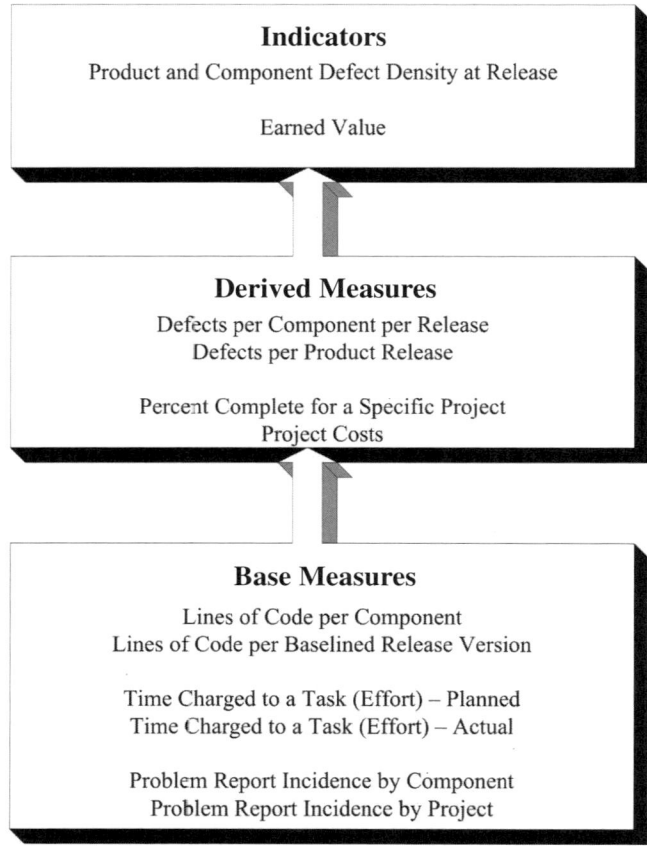

Figure 2-3 ● Sample Architecture based on ISO/IEC 15939

Of course, there's much more to a measurement effort than collecting some data and putting it in charts. Measurement is a service. The measurement effort needs to deliver its messages effectively, accurately, and in a timely fashion. Most important, it needs to satisfy the end user's information needs.

The best way to work out both the technical and the service-side details of the measurement effort is to fully analyze your current needs and goals as well as those of future, anticipated stakeholders in the effort. This analysis phase involves the following steps:

1. Identify when and where you will take measurements. These are the measurement locations or measurement points.
2. Based on the measurement points, determine the measurement details (such as level of granularity and measurement type).
3. Establish the measurement architecture.
4. Determine what tools or infrastructure will be required to support the effort.

Step 1: Identify When, Where, and What to Measure

You'll expect your measures to tell you three things:

1. Are we done with this part of the project?
2. Did we do a good job up to this point?
3. What risks, if any, remain?

Select Locations

To answer these questions, you'll want to select measurement locations that give you the best visibility into the project. Typically these locations are interfaces, impact points, and milestones:

- *Interfaces* are where work products are delivered, exchanged, and/or reviewed.
- *Impact points* are where and when a work product is first used or where and when an event is first noticed or its effects are first felt.
- *Milestones* are interim completion points, where work products are reviewed and handed over to another group or where collections of tasks are completed and need to be reviewed for status and quality.

So your first task is to identify the interfaces between groups and the boundaries between phases. Next, determine when changes are made to the work products (e.g., specifications, user manuals, code). Finally, think about when these changes may have their first impact on different parts of the organization, because changes may be made long before anyone detects the changes (or needs to detect them).

Select Event or Impact

Whether you want to instrument the act of the change or when the change first impacts another part of the organization depends on what you are measuring and whether the event or the impact is most important.

For example, most source code control tools will give you a daily report of code-level changes. Is it important for you to know the daily change rate or just to audit each build to determine changes to total lines of code? Will the test organization need to know the daily rates or is it really only affected by the builds and thus only cares about the build total?

Choosing between measuring events or impact is often a matter of common sense. If you are looking at the requirements management cycle, little may be gained from knowing how many times a requirement changes during the initial negotiations with the customer. However, it is worth knowing how many changes occur after the final requirements acceptance review, because these changes can impact productivity, released product quality, and schedule compliance.

Set Boundaries

In a few cases it is necessary to set boundaries arbitrarily, such as when you are tracking defects to determine defect density or phase containment. When the boundaries between test phases are always shifting, you may have to make arbitrary decisions about when a phase is over and when to review the data for that phase. As long as the criteria for the end date are the same across releases and projects, the phase containment data will be consistent enough to be useful. Pre-release defect density or containment is fairly easy to calculate once you have established whether the release date is the start of a beta or acceptance test, the end of the installation warranty period, or maybe even the date the product is released from the testing organization.

It's a bit harder to determine milestones and impact points for software that has been released. For example, post-release defect density and the total of released defects for containment calculations require some seemingly arbitrary decisions about measurement points. Defect data from customer sites may be delayed because installations take place at multiple sites over a period of months or even years.

Customer use of the product also is a contributing factor. If a customer installs the product but only uses 30 percent of its functionality for the first year, this can skew your defect data. It may be necessary to set an arbitrary cut-off date—say six months after the product ships or one month before the next major version ships—and calculate released defect density based on the data extant at the time.

Step 2: Determine the Details

Next to where to measure, the most important decision you must make is how to collect the data to make it most credible.

Data Sources

Will the data be collected from a utility, from interviewing people, from spur-of-the-moment conversations with project team members, or from a combination of these and other sources? These sources vary in accuracy and availability, but you may need to use all of them at some point in your measurement effort. Even with a very sophisticated problem-report tracking system, it is usually necessary to get input from developers or testers to interpret some of the data (e.g., when a fix to one problem uncovers or causes several other problems).

Knowing the source of the data will help you decide if you have to adjust your measurement methods to take subjectivity and filtering into account. Will you be working with data that has already been reviewed and processed by someone else? Problem reports coming from the field that pass through second-level support may have new information added to them, or they may have been edited. Does it matter if you have the original report or a filtered one? Can your tracking tool keep both the original and the processed versions?

As for subjectivity, very few measures in software don't have a subjective component. For example, is a requirements change really a change or is it just a case of getting the requirement right the second time around? Are all problem reports to be counted as defects, or just some subset? There's no such thing as a design failure *per se*—it's always code that fails—so when is a code defect not a defect at all but the correct implementation of a bad design?

Filtering and subjectivity are best dealt with through standardizing data reporting. Problem severity should have only three or four possible values, and these should be enforced with a tool. Usability should have some quantifiable component (e.g., tasks completed per minute) and a scaled rating system for the user evaluation (e.g., performance is poor [1] or excellent [5]). The key steps in managing subjectively and filtering are:

1. Establish a process for recording data.
2. Use a form that calls for specific information.
3. Require descriptions of events or steps rather than impressions.
4. Constrain the possible values of subjective impression data.

Level of Granularity

For everything you want to measure, determine all the attributes of the entities being measured. Then look at the interrelationships between attributes and the mechanisms for collecting the data. Specifically, you will need to identify:

➡ All possible relationships between attributes
➡ Any causal relationships (verifiable or hypothetical) between attributes
➡ The means by which the data is collected and whether that determines the type of measure (incidence, diagnostic, heuristic)
➡ Whether the choice of type of measure constrains what derived measures or indicators can legitimately be used.

You will not want to measure every one of these attributes or relationships. Knowing how the pieces fit, however, will help you understand what pieces you want to pay attention to. This exercise will also help you determine the level of granularity you want to achieve with your measures.

For example, suppose we want to measure customer problem reports. Analyzing customer problems, we find that an error report may have multiple causes and attributes. In the example in Figure 2-4, defects leading to customer-visible errors have been divided into six categories: code-level defects, error-handling deficiencies, design failures, stress- or load-related failures, platform incompatibilities, and problems with requirements. These are also the main causes for customer-visible errors.

Each category has specific attributes. For example, some code-level defects may be due to errors in algorithms or reused patterns. Error recovery can fail because context is lost between threads. Requirements can be defective because they are ambiguous or because one requirement conflicts with another.

Which of the attributes in Figure 2-4 do we want to measure? Where in the lifecycle would it be best to measure them? Can they be measured in the same way, for example, through the defect tracking tool? Or do they need different types of collection methods? What level of granularity is appropriate? Do we need to dissect defects to the lowest attribute level, or will the category level be sufficient?

If you plan to diagnose process problems with your product defect data, you will want a finer level of granularity than if you simply want to establish some product ship criteria. In the former case, you'll want to distinguish defects at the attribute level, since this data will help you plan future testing and guide future designs. For ship criteria, you will probably want to distinguish errors in functions from platform-related failures, focusing primarily on incidence rates rather than on root causes or typologies.

Type: Incidence, Diagnostic, or Heuristic?

Some measures tell you something about the state of a product or a process, or they show that some event has occurred. These are incidence measures, such as lines of code, number of defects, etc.

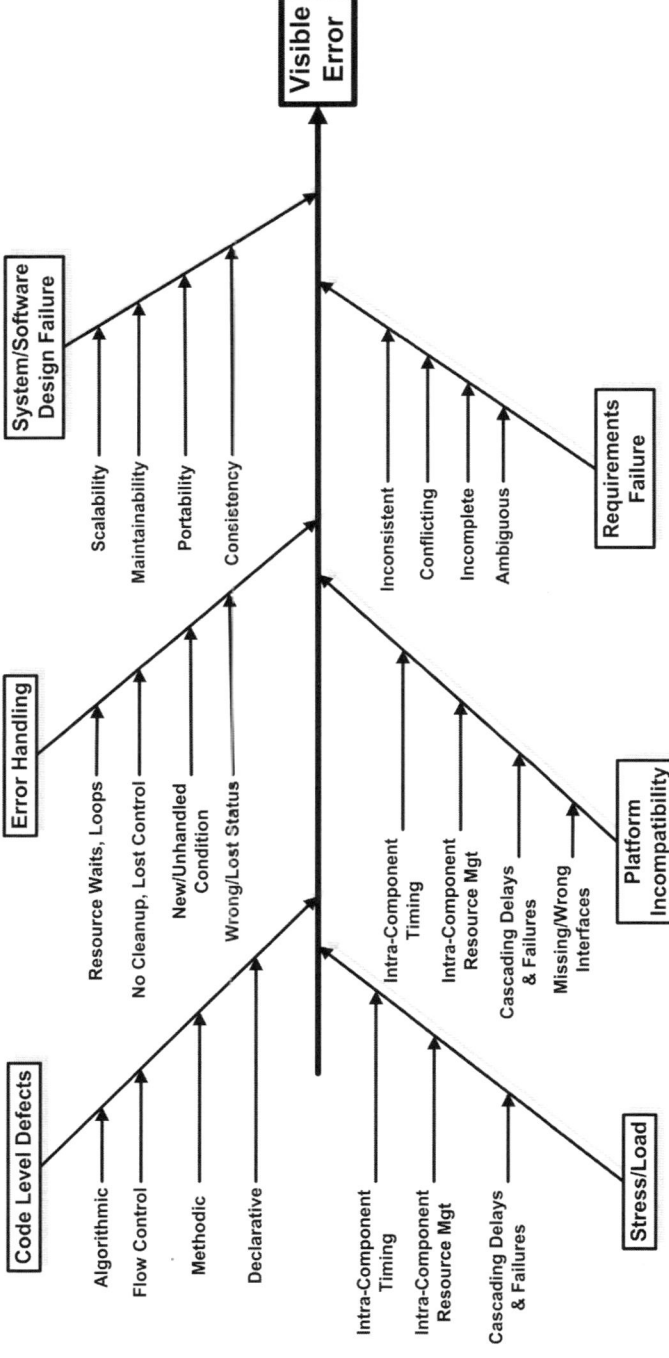

Figure 2-4 ■ Categories, Causes, and Attributes of Customer-Visible Errors

Other measurements tell you something about why the product is in that state or point out causal relationships. These are diagnostic measures, such as injection phase or root cause.

Some measures (especially those that are subjective or are based on multiple attributes) give you insight into a product, process, or event and help you evaluate the situation. These are heuristic measures, such as problem severity, customer priority, or usability rating.

Distinguishing between measurement types is important because it will affect your choice of models, indicators, and decision criteria. A diagnostic measure, properly conceived, can be turned very easily into an indicator and won't require additional measurement data. A heuristic measure, on the other hand, will by its very nature require other measurement data when it is rolled up into an indicator.

What About End-of-Life Projects?

If your organization develops and maintains several versions of the same product, it's partly a business decision about which of these need measurement attention. There's probably no business reason to implement a full-scale measurement effort on a product that is going to be moved to end-of-life in six months. However, you may want to have some data from such a project to be used as a benchmark or to help put other project data in the proper context.

For example, when a new product replaces an old one, but uses some of the original code base, it's a good idea to have root-cause and defect-by-component profiles from the previous product to help you assess data on the new one. Keep in mind that for financial or legal reasons you may have to exclude products from measurement (such as a legacy system in pay-per-request maintenance mode).

Step 3: Establish the Architecture

Software measurement is evolutionary. What you want to know today may be only a fraction of what you want to know in one or two years. Take, for example, the notion of severity and priority in problem reporting. Most commercial and home-grown problem management utilities provide a way to identify the severity and priority of a problem (e.g., high-medium-low, critical-major-minor). Some organizations use severity to measure the defect's impact on the customer and priority to indicate how quickly the development organization needs to fix the problem.

Both of these are fairly coarse indicators, even when we ignore their subjective component. Neither measure accounts for such considerations as the complexity of the fix, its potential for destabilizing other segments of the product, the degree to which all customers are exposed to the defect and the frequency of its occurrence on the exposed sites, and the impact on the project in time and effort used to fix the problem and to test the fix.

Base Measures

Start with as wide a range of base measures as possible to make room for new requirements from your stakeholders and for the evolution of your information needs. Sooner or later you will need measurements of:

- *Size.* The physical or logical size of the product (e.g., lines of code, function points, classes and class hierarchies).
- *Complexity.* Sometimes defined as the size of the product measured in units such as lines of source code. Can also be measured by the number of requirements or interfaces, or by commercial functional complexity tools.
- *Effort.* Defined as direct labor time and/or elapsed time to complete a task, usually measured in person hours.
- *Capability or performance.* Initially measured as tasks completed (planned vs. actual) and conformance to schedule.
- *Product quality.* Initially based on number and types of defects.
- *Process capability.* Usually based on defects found per development phase, change requests, etc.

Derived Measures

With a solid foundation of base measures, derived measures are easily expanded to meet your needs. Plan for the incremental implementation of more (and more advanced) derived measures. An organization that is still learning to use defect run rates to determine readiness to ship is probably not ready to embrace residual defect calculations (such as those used in the Personal Software Process[SM]). Options for derived measures are discussed in detail in Chapters 3 and 4.

Models and Indicators

Models and indicators are the interface between raw measures and the information needs of the user community. A "hierarchy of needs" must usually be met. Line managers need information that will help them guide their projects in real time. Quality personnel are likely to want to see process-level trends and occasionally product-level detail. Senior management will want all of this rolled up into time and cost. Selecting models and indicators can be as much a political balancing act as it is a technical task.

Perhaps the best example of a politically charged indicator is defect density. In some organizations, defect density is never discussed. Senior management doesn't want to know how many defects there are in the product. In their view, the software will be defect-free at shipment or someone will be fired. This is not the kind of environment where you can generate a defect density chart for the past three releases and present it at the next business operations review. Even if your density data makes you a world-class development team, you might just as well put your resignation letter up on the screen instead.

Even when the environment is more sympathetic toward software's notorious deficiencies, engineering management may object to your use of a measure that can be so easily misconstrued. They might argue, and rightly so, that defect density takes on a different meaning depending on when it is calculated in the development project. A high defect density at release time may mean that the testing organization was particularly thorough in its testing and the customer base will never experience any significant problems with the software. A low defect density at release time may mean there was insufficient time to test the product, but it might also mean that informal peer reviews of the design and code were so effective at removing defects that very few made it into the test and acceptance phases.

The case of low defect density is particularly interesting. Is it a defect in the indicator that you can't tell the difference between a "good" low value and a "bad" one? Suppose the informal peer reviews really were that effective? Isn't that something we'd want to measure? Wouldn't we want to use that data to help us understand the significance of the defect density at the end of the test period? So where does the problem lie, in the indicator or in the model used to calculate it? In the model, of course: all defect data should be factored into a defect density calculation.

This is not only good measurement, but also good corporate citizenship. Why shouldn't the developers get credit for all their hard work in reviewing out product defects? If there are some political jitters about showing how many defects the work products contain, the project manager can always compare the effort involved in reviews versus test. When the senior management team sees that peer reviews are very effective at reducing defect fix cycles in the test phase, maybe they'll support the project managers in their other process improvement efforts.

Step 4: Identify Tools and Infrastructure Requirements

Development teams often identify new measurements they would like to have, only to discover that their current tools can't capture all the data they want and/or can't report the data. It makes sense to start with what you have and build from there. Microsoft Office tools are certainly good enough for starters, and a number of relatively inexpensive add-ins are available for calculating and charting. From there you can move toward any of the commercially available metrics packages.

Whatever you do, plan the effort out in phases to provide incremental enhancements that will minimize implementation costs and new technology risks. After all, you don't want to destabilize current collection and reporting processes during the introduction of enhancements!

As your measurement program matures, you will want to have access to historical data for projects. Minimally, you'll need storage space, an appropriately designed archival database, and possibly a reporting tool. Have the database developers help design an archival system that will support your current, real-time reporting but also make historical trend and multi-attribute reporting possible.

● A TYPICAL MEASUREMENT IMPLEMENTATION

To illustrate the measurement architecture discussed, let's look at the components of a typical software measurement program.

Base Measures

Typical base measures include:

- Number of defects, usually counted as number of problem reports
- Time charged, estimated and actual
- Cost, actual and estimated
- Size, usually expressed as lines of code or number of function points.

Some of the base measures have attributes that are also measured:

- *Defect status.* Reflects the progress that has been made in remedying the defect.
- *Defects per component.* The number of defects in some subcategory of the product, such as system architectural components, source projects or files, etc.
- *Defect injection phase.* Identifies when the defect was created.
- *Defect detection phase.* Identifies when the defect was discovered.
- *Direct labor time (or cost).*
- *Appraisal and prevention time (or cost).* The time spent in identifying defects and preventing defects in the first place.

Derived Measures

These base measures are combined with each other at various project phases and milestones to provide a set of derived measures. Some of these derived measures are simply incidence measures. Others, such as injection phase, have diagnostic value. And some, such as size, can be used heuristically. The typical combinations are:

- Number of defects per build
- Number of defects per project milestone
- Number of defects per release

- Defect status per build
- Defect status per project milestone
- Defect status per release

- Injection phase of defects per build
- Injection phase of defects per project milestone
- Injection phase of defects per release

- Estimated duration per task
- Actual duration per task
- Estimated duration per project phase
- Actual duration per project phase
- Estimated duration for complete project
- Actual duration for complete project
- Estimated direct labor per task
- Actual direct labor per task
- Estimated direct labor per project phase
- Actual direct labor per project phase
- Estimated direct labor for complete project
- Actual direct labor for complete project

- Size per build and difference from baseline
- Size per release.

Indicators

The derived measures are combined with each other to create performance indicators. These indicators are normally used in advanced metrics programs that have data for many projects over several years. However, they have heuristic value even when used in one or two projects.

These indicators are:

- *Phase containment.* The ability of the development processes to remove defects in the current phase and not release them into subsequent phases. Usually expressed as the number or percent of defects detected in one segment of a project compared to the total known number of defects.
- *Defect density.* The number of defects in the product per some standard unit of size measurement (e.g., defects per 1,000 lines of source code).
- *Earned value.* A way of combining effort, tasks, and cost to determine percent completion on a project schedule.
- *Cost of quality/cost of poor quality.* The cost of appraisal tasks and the cost to detect and remove defects.

Software project management is particularly challenging because so many aspects of software development are interrelated. Requirements specificity affects the precision of the design as well as test coverage. The platform for the product affects the speed with which code can be developed as well as the kinds of quality risks introduced in the coding effort. Similarly, software measures are interrelated. A measure that by itself is just an incidence measure can be used heuristically if it is combined with other information from the project.

For example, the number of defects can be tracked by build, by project milestone, or by release. These are derived measures of incidence. Combining the derived measure of defect rate for several releases of the same product, at the same project milestones, gives us the phase containment indicator. This indicator is also itself an incidence measure. It tells us what the trend is and identifies where there may be variations. Without additional information, we can't diagnose the cause of the variations from the run rates alone. To perform root cause analysis, we would need to draw upon some of the other measures, such as defect injection phase, defect detection phase, and lines of code.

Chapters 3, 4, and 5 will explain these measures in more detail and show you how to use them to manage software development.

● APPLYING WHAT YOU'VE LEARNED

The following exercises will lead you through establishing some of the requirements for your measurement effort.

Exercise 2-1: Identifying Information Needs

Initially, you will be the primary customer of your measurement data. To use the results of your measurements effectively, however, you will have to convey that data in ways your management can appreciate. As your effort matures, other departments may become stakeholders in your data. So it is important to know from the outset how your measurement goals fit in with the goals of the rest of the company. Answering the following questions will help you position your effort in the larger corporate framework.

1. In Chapter 1, you identified some of your company values.
   a. Which of these already have measurements associated with them?
   b. Are these measurements adequate? Do they properly represent your challenges and successes?
   c. Are these measurements accurate? Are they appropriate for your project environment and will they reveal appropriate and useful information about your project performance?
2. In Chapter 1, you identified the explicit or implicit business goals for your department.
   a. Which of these already have measurements associated with them?
   b. Are these measurements incidental, diagnostic, or heuristic?
   c. Are they adequate?
   d. Are they accurate?
3. Identify the current or future stakeholders in your measurement information.
   a. Who would benefit from it?

b. Who might want to have input into what is being measured?

c. Who would want to review your results?

d. Are there any people in your organization who should *not* see your data?

Exercise 2-2: Learning from History

Another way to determine what you need in a measurement effort is to review old project plans and think about what went awry in the projects:

1. What information do you now wish you had then for making decisions about how to correct the problems?
2. What information do you now wish you had then for making risk assessments?
3. How can you obtain this information in the upcoming project?

Exercise 2-3: Approaching Measurement as Risk Mitigation

We have focused on defects and time as the key operational measures. Product quality issues, schedule slips, and productivity problems are typically the main drivers of software project risks. However, it is certainly possible to approach your measurement effort solely as a risk mitigation effort. Thinking of measures as risk mitigation tools helps put the numbers in perspective.

1. Select three or four categories of development activities that suit your development culture and lifecycle.
2. For each of these categories, identify and group the tasks typically required in that category.
3. By category or by group, identify any risks to successful completion of the tasks.
4. From the risk analysis, identify the attributes of the tasks and/or their environment that you will want to monitor.
5. Determine the appropriate unit of measurement and when you will measure these attributes.

6. Write down any rules for measuring the data or guidelines for its interpretation.

Exercise 2-4: Selecting a Strategy and an Implementation Plan

Answer the following questions to initiate the implementation planning for your measurement effort:

1. What will the focus be for this measurement effort: time, defects, or risk?
2. What segments of the development lifecycle or project lifecycle need to be measured?
3. At what times/phases/places should measurements be made?
4. Will the data be collected from a single source or multiple sources? Will some of the data be filtered data?
5. Given the collection points and the amount of data available, do you expect your measures to be incidence measures, diagnostic measures, or heuristic measures?

CHAPTER

3

Applying the Basics: Run Rates

Managing performance *within* a project rather than the performance *of* a project requires you to probe beneath work breakdown structure (WBS) items to the surrounding events and influences. It is not enough to know that the design for feature XYZ is 75 percent complete; you need to know what "complete" really means. For example:

➤ Has 75 percent of the allocated time been used?
➤ Are the technical aspects of the design three-quarters complete?
➤ Is the documentation task (writing, reviewing, etc.) three-quarters complete?

The issue here is whether the task has met its obligations to the rest of the project. The WBS merely identifies tasks associated with tangible deliverables. It's not enough to know that Task X is "done." As a project manager, you need to know what impact those deliverables will have on other project staff downstream in the development process.

Let's take a very simple, but telling, example. Suppose that the development team has just completed the requirements specification for a major component in the release you are managing. On your project plan, the WBS item is now 100 percent. If the specification was completed on the planned date, your project is on schedule. If the specification was completed with the planned number of resources and effort hours, your project is on track with respect to resource allocation and cost. Looks good, so far.

But any error in that requirement specification puts at risk some other task later in the project. We all know that in software development projects, errors propagate. Seemingly small problems can cascade down the task item list, growing more serious and increasing your risks as they go. An ambiguously stated requirement leads to an incorrect design choice. The incorrect design choice results in coded functions that are not fully compatible with the rest of the required functions. This problem isn't discovered until the project has entered the system test phase, when it is expensive to fix the problem and the fix involves high risks.

Unfortunately, unless you have a very disciplined development environment, you can't assess how well a task has met its obligations to the rest of the project until sometime after the task has been completed. Moreover, you can't recognize cascading errors unless you look at the project over time. This is why run rate measurements are essential for software project management. Typical run rate measures include defect discovery rates, problem report closure rates, task completion rates, and effort expenditure rates. While these attributes of the project can't tell you everything you might want to know about how your project is going "on the ground," they will give you some insight into the effect of any given task, deliverable, or event.

● PROCEED WITH CAUTION

Nonetheless, run rates must be used carefully. They are merely incidence measures. Incidence measures tell you that some event occurred: a defect was discovered, a task has been completed. Incidence measures can't tell you anything about the cause of the event. They reveal little about the conditions under which the event occurred. Lacking the whole picture, you can easily jump to wrong conclusions.

For example, logically speaking, the number of defects *per se* is not a particularly good indicator of product quality unless you have control over the conditions under which defects can be injected and discovered. A high level of defects isn't usually problematic. If the product is full of bugs, in most cases it's safe to assume that the product is low quality. (Whether it can be shipped in that state is a different question.) The logical quandary comes when few defects are discovered. Does a low defect rate indicate that the product contains only a small number of errors? Or does it only tell us that a low number of defects has been discovered?

Manufacturing environments are very good at constraining the source and frequency of defect injections. They also have specific criteria and methods for determining defects. If a product is created under controlled conditions such that it is made exactly the same way every time, the introduction of defects is constrained. That is, there is a set of identifiable, consistently present conditions under which a defect can be introduced into the product.

If the product is also evaluated (tested) in the same way every time, the domain of possible defects is constrained. In other words, the method of evaluation forces us to look at one set of attributes, not every possible attribute. Under these two constraints, we can draw legitimate (if not absolute) conclusions from low defect detection rates.

Whether software development can ever achieve the manufacturing sector's level of consistency and legitimacy has been debated for decades. Plenty of evidence shows that organizations that use a quality management system driven by the CMMI® model or the IEEE standards have a better chance at constraining defect injections and determining residual risk. The standardizations that these systems provide limit to some extent the variation in the data, which in turn helps simplify and legitimize interpretations of that data. But there's also plenty of psychological and sociological research indicating that on a day-to-day basis, at a person-to-person level, projects are more like organic complex systems than they are like manufacturing lines.

The fact that the debate over software process control remains unresolved is a warning not to draw hasty conclusions from measurements. Measures are tools. You have to know how and when to use them. Perhaps more important, your skill in using them will improve with experience over time. To fully understand quantitative data, you have to have qualitative background information. You need to know how the project team behaves under normal and under stressful conditions. You should understand enough about the software development process to appreciate it as a workflow, an exchange of information, and a series of interrelated decisions.

Quantitative software project management is one part numbers and two parts reflection on the significance of the numbers. Most software metrics books focus on the numbers and how to manipulate them. Most of the rest of this book focuses on how to reflect on the data and how to extract from it insights into the current and future health of your project. Your decisions will not have the same logical force as those derived from statistical process control. But they don't need to: they only have to be good enough to get you over the next obstacle. (If you have questions about the methodological validity of such reflections, see Appendix A.)

● THE KEY ATTRIBUTES OF DEFECTS AND TIME

For most software projects, the essential attributes to measure are defects and time. Defect-related measures examine attributes of the product and are usually tied to problem reports or configuration items such as builds or releases. Defect-related base measures don't carry much significance by themselves, and projects typically use derived measures combining defects and time.

Time-related measures are focused on aspects of processes or projects, telling you how long it takes to complete specific tasks. Unlike defect base measures, these base measures often can stand on their own, as in comparing planned time with actual time. (Cost measures, where time is expressed in monetary units rather than hours or days, are discussed in Chapter 5.)

Defects and time have important sub-attributes. Defects can be categorized by their state, injection phase, or detection phase. For time, there's estimated time, actual time, and other types based on the types of tasks involved. To use these measures effectively, you need to know what they can and cannot tell you about your project, and you need to know when to use them.

● DEFECTS, DEFECTS, EVERYWHERE

You walk up to your new car in the mall parking lot and discover that your driver's door has been scratched slightly while you were inside shopping. Maybe the passenger in the car parked next to you did it when he or she opened the car door. Maybe someone brushed up against your door as they walked by, and their studded belt or purse scraped the paint. How the scratch got there isn't important to you. All you know is that your new car has been marred and that you are annoyed. After a minute's thought, though, you realize that the scratch is repairable. All you need to do is to apply a little touch-up paint when you get home and your car will be as good as new.

What does this have to do with software defects? We tend to think of software defects in the same way: they are unpleasant little discoveries that can be fixed quickly and simply. But not all defects can be fixed quickly or simply. Some can't be fixed at all. What's more, behind every defect in the product is a corresponding defect or deficiency in the process used to make the product. Defect reports coming out of the test lab aren't just superficial scratches on the outside of your new product. They reflect problems in requirements, design, coding, or even project management.

What Is a Product Defect?

There are probably as many answers to the question of what a product defect is as there are developers, testers, and users of your product. Even when the product requirements have been precisely captured and exactly implemented, there's always someone who takes exception to what the product does or how quickly and easily it does it. The best way to deal with this diversity of opinion is to use a broad definition of defect and then to refine that definition with defect types in the measurements.

For our purposes we'll use "defect" to mean any documented problem with a product. The rationale for this broad definition is simply this: if someone has taken the time to document an issue with the product, then some amount of your project time and resources has been spent (or will be spent) dealing with that issue.

Problem reports that turn out to be due to the customer mis-understanding how the product functions are just "noise" as far as Change Control Boards and development engineers are concerned. From the project perspective, however, no matter how insignificant the problem was, they represent lost productivity. A development project can be put at risk by an abundance of noise reports just as easily as it can be put at risk by one or two reports of system crashes.

What Is a Process Defect?

In a high-maturity organization with a fully implemented Software Quality Assurance program, not performing formal code inspections is a process defect. In a low-maturity organization, not allocating enough time for testing is a process defect. The simplest answer to the question of what is a process defect is probably: anything that increases your risks.

With this definition, process defects would include neglecting to get stakeholder approvals, not performing requirements reviews, or tracking resource time at too high a level of granularity. Whether something is a process defect or an opportunity for improvement is up to you and your common sense. For example, formal code inspections are a proven technique for lowering your defect rates, but they are expensive in terms of both time and resources. If there's no time in your current project plan allocated to code inspections, you'd probably put your project at greater risk by implementing inspections on the fly. Chalk inspections up to a future process improvement, not a process defect.

How to Use Defect Run Rates

Run rates are derived measures. They combine the number of defects with some time period. They are typically used to identify trends—for example, the defect rate is rising or falling. Many organizations also use defect run rates as a quality indicator: if the rate of newly discovered defects drops just before the release date, the product is good to go. Logically speaking, this is a misuse of the measure: the defect discovery rate is an attribute of the test process, not of the quality of the product. In fact, run rates can be used to measure process efficiency as well as to measure events.

Run rates can be computed as current counts or as running totals. Current counts are the current number of defects per some category per some time period. At each time period, the current number of defects is recorded. Figure 3-1 displays current counts. On each day, the number of problem reports in the new state is calculated, and that daily number is added to the chart. Current counts are typically used for daily or weekly trend analysis and for transition states in a process where, after the transition, there's no trace of the previous state.

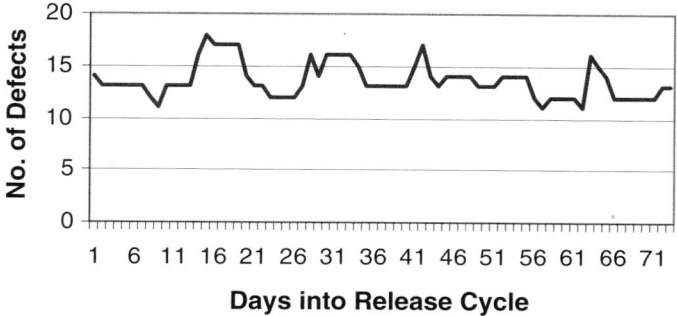

Figure 3-1 ■ Sample Current Count Defect Rate Chart

On the other hand, running totals are typically used when the attribute of interest is an end state of a process—total number of problem reports closed to date, total number of tasks completed to date, etc. For current totals, the number of defects in a particular category is determined for the current and all previous time periods. In Figure 3-2, the current total is used to show the increase in the number of issues closed during a release.

Interpreting Defect Run Rate Data

Run rates are subject to many influences, and can be interpreted in different, sometimes conflicting ways. Peaks, trends, and troughs in the data aren't self-explanatory. To appreciate the real significance of the lines, you have to examine the data in the context of the project events that produced the data.

Figure 3-3 illustrates defect incidence over time for a release. The chart uses current counts of the number of new or unprocessed problem reports per day. A new problem report is considered a new defect. New problem reports that are not processed into some other state (e.g., opened for review) are included in the subsequent day's count.

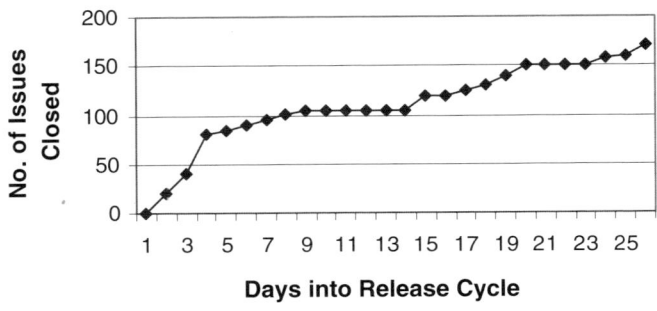

Figure 3-2 ● Sample Running Total Defect Rate Chart

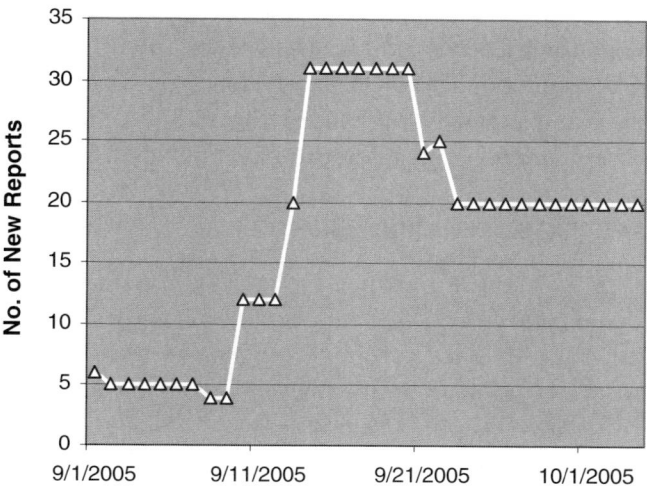

Figure 3-3 ● Example of a Defect Run Rate Chart

While the chart shows trends in the data, it doesn't help us understand what those trends mean. There's no way to determine from this data alone why the defect rate peaks between 9/10/2005 and 9/16/2005, or why the rate drops around the 9/22/2005 mark. The chart doesn't help us understand why the rate levels off around 9/25/2005, or why that level is so much higher than the rate earlier in the month. Nor does the chart tell us why the new defect rate has remained constant for the last several days.

It could be that there's some kind of delay in the Change Control Board and it cannot process all the reports. Or perhaps the development team doesn't consider the defects important, so the reports are languishing on the "new" list. Or maybe the test team has hit some obstacle and can't test the product any further, so the trend line really reflects a productivity problem in the test lab.

Thus, defect incidence by itself is not a useful measure unless you view the data in the context of the project as a whole. That context includes any events that might have affected the data and any direct causes for the data points themselves. In Chapter 4 we will look at some defect attributes that can help you diagnose the cause of the defect and assess its risks. For the moment, it's important to understand how defect run rates can be affected by project events.

● PROJECT EVENTS AFFECTING RUN RATES

Since project milestones are typically integrated with development lifecycle milestones, it is important to recognize what effects the development lifecycle can have on your defect data. The development lifecycle model will affect your defect measurement points as well as the rates you experience.

In a waterfall development model, requirements are established before design begins, and coding completes before testing begins. You would normally measure defect rates at the completion of these phases in the development effort. Typically, you would expect to see a steady decrease in the defect rates as the development effort progresses. (In some circumstances an increase in defect rate is due to a planned event, such as use of a particular requirements generation method or a change in test approach.)

On the other hand, iterative development models combine requirements, design, coding, and testing into several mini-cycles or iterations. Some iterative models involve the customer throughout the development iterations; others do not. The crucial difference between the linear waterfall model and the cyclic iterative models is their approach to product validation and their view of defects.

In the waterfall model, testing is expected to validate the complete product. Defects are "expected" only in the sense that software always exhibits defects. Of course, a high incidence of defect reports is never really good news.

In contrast, iterative models take seriously the old adage that customers don't really know what they want the software to do until they see it. It's not uncommon in iterative development models to "turn the customer loose" on a prototype as a way of iteratively defining the requirements. At the end of such an iteration, a high defect incidence rate is actually good news, because it indicates that the customer is using and evaluating the product.

Regardless of the development model, some project events will affect your defect rate data.

Static and Dynamic Test Approaches

Peer reviews and unit testing should eliminate design flaws, algorithmic flaws, and resource utilization failures. If these activities have been performed properly, functional testing is unlikely to generate many defects, but platform integration, system test, and load/stress testing may. No spikes at first is not necessarily good news.

If these have been performed and the first test build shows a high incidence of issues in these areas, several possibilities need to be investigated. For example, the peer reviews were done on code that was subsequently changed, they were careless, or there's a configuration management problem because the build apparently didn't pick up the properly peer-reviewed code.

A *change in the test approach* can either increase or decrease the coverage of the testing. Early in the test cycle, functional testing normally takes precedence; unless peer reviews and detailed unit testing are performed, this approach to testing normally generates the highest level of defects in the test period. At the other end of the test cycle, be wary of the period when the test team switches from requirements validation to ad hoc testing. Ad hoc testing stresses the system beyond its documented requirements and limits, often generating a high number of problem reports. Not all these reports may be significant for the release, depending upon the requirements and the ship criteria.

The ideal situation is to see the defects rates drop as testing proceeds. That said, rate decreases need to be interpreted from the standpoints of the test approach and the particular test target. For example, regression testing is less likely to reveal defects than ad hoc or exploratory testing. If regression testing takes up the last half of a test cycle, the decrease is to be expected but may not indicate that all new defects have been removed. Conversely, if at the end of a test cycle there's been a flurry of debugging and retesting activity for one software component, you might see a late peak in the defect discovery rate followed by an immediate drop. In this case, because of the type of testing involved, there's a good chance you have removed the new, latent defects.

Dynamic Test Events

If unit test defects are logged, the *start of unit test* will likely be accompanied by an increase in the defect counts. If people outside your group see this spike, they may think that there's a quality problem. That may be true, but defects in unit test can't be properly interpreted without some additional information: the nature of the tests, their coverage, and the time developers have had to code the units.

If unit testing is planned and the plans are peer-reviewed, you can assume that the tests are methodical and address key functions of the unit. Based on these assumptions, you can provisionally conclude that a lack of spikes means that the unit testing is going well. It's never over until it's over, so there's still the chance that the initial tests go smoothly and subsequent ones fail. But a spike in defect reports may indicate that development didn't have enough time to work through the coding phase. There is still *some* good news: the defects are being discovered early, when there's ample time to fix them and the risk of maintenance errors is small.

If there are no unit test plans and there's no other way to determine the depth and coverage of unit testing, then you do not have any additional insight into what a spike or lack of a spike means. When you first start measuring defects at this measurement point, assume that a "quiet" unit test period means that the testing is not finding the defects it should and these will appear later in the cycle. After you have some experience with defect rates here and later in the cycle, you may be able to use historical trends to determine whether a quiet unit test phase will or will not have an impact later in the cycle.

When testing on new platforms or testing new components, expect spikes to occur at the *start of integration testing*. Once again, you'll need some historical data and some insight into the development effort to interpret the actual run rates.

For example, suppose you are integrating code developed in-house with code from an external vendor or contract house. Unless you have excellent supplier management, your first few days in the test lab are likely to be challenging. This is to be expected (and because it is to be expected, the project schedule should include time for it!).

In the absence of historical data, always take a slow start to defect run rates in integration testing as an invitation to look deeper into what's happening. It may be that the hardware wasn't ready on time or didn't work as expected. It may be that the test team was still coming up to speed on the functionality and didn't hit the ground running. It may be that the components to be integrated are a match made in heaven and the project will finish three weeks ahead of schedule. In any case, these are factors you want to know about to help you properly apply the current data heuristically in the next cycle.

Assuming that all committed functionality and code is ready in the first build, a *spike in the first build* is likely. Spikes in the defect discovery rate in mid- to late-cycle need to be analyzed for root causes.

Sometimes, developers will fix one problem and the fix will uncover one or more problems. Sometimes a fix will break other functionality (a.k.a., a bad fix). These produce *cascading failures*, whereby testing one fix generates more defect reports. These cascading failures can be time-consuming for developers and testers and need to be monitored. Often, this can't be done with defect run rates because these cascading failures contribute a small number of defects to the total daily or weekly rate. Moreover, component-level defect rates may not show the cascade, since the subsequent defects don't necessarily show up in the same components. This is one of those cases where quantitative analysis alone will fail without some "management by walking around."

Time Period for Release Phases

Short development cycles will usually require iterative development and/or abbreviated testing (unit through systems), with a corresponding decrease in coverage and detail of testing. If you have planned, focused, and coordinated the testing throughout all its phases, then low run rates can be an indication of product quality. If you have injection phase data for the defects, it is worth cross-referencing the rates with the injection phase to determine whether there are some weaknesses in the coverage. For example, coding defects late in the system test cycle are an indication that the unit and integration testing was probably not comprehensive enough. There may be more latent defects than you expected.

There's a peculiar irony in *long development cycles*. Developers and testers welcome longer cycles so they have plenty of time to do the job right. On the other hand, there's the risk of habituation. If the longer cycle includes intermittent builds for occasional testing, the test team may extract many defects before the formal test period starts. Lack of a spike at the first formal test build may mean that the code is clean.

On the other hand, it may also mean that the test team is habituated to the same testing and isn't probing the product deeply enough. During long release cycles, teams adjust to take the paths of least resistance. Code that has been tested once may receive only cursory functionality checks rather than full testing in subsequent builds. No news is not necessarily good news in this case.

● WHAT DO YOU MEAN, YOU AREN'T DONE YET?

Someone who sits in the project manager's chair probably thinks of time tracking as nothing more than estimating how long it will take to complete some task and then determining how long it actually took to complete the task. Someone who sits in a developer's chair likely thinks of time tracking as a naive and impracticable requirement. Rarely do developers get to spend 100 percent of their days on their assigned tasks. They've learned to work on their assigned tasks in the blocks of time between meetings, support calls, and development environment maintenance. In the developer's world, there is a difference between elapsed time (the time between task start and finish on your project plan) and their actual direct labor time on the task.

Your time measurements need to make the same distinction. After selecting the tasks you want to monitor, estimate the time to complete the task both in direct labor hours and in duration or elapsed time from starting the task to finishing it. When the task is completed, determine the actual direct labor time and the actual duration. You may also want to account from the outset for discrepancies between estimated and actual time. Identify the various causes for discrepancies and choose which ones you'd like to watch for.

That can be challenging. Software projects are notorious for being over budget and late in delivery. That's not surprising when you consider the number of things that can adversely affect both the schedule and the cost. The typical practice of putting 10–15 percent of the estimated project costs into a contingency fund is fine if the adverse influences can be controlled. But the sheer number of such influences is daunting. Figure 3-4 catalogues just a few of the reasons why actual time may exceed estimated time for tasks in your project.

Your estimates can accommodate some of these factors, such as padding the time required for customer turnaround of the deliverables or leaving extra time at the end of the development cycle as contingency against requirements changes. On the other hand, some of these factors have to be monitored in real time, such as developer interruptions, rework, and testing problems. This not only lets you take corrective action in that particular instance, but it also provides you with data you can use in estimations for future projects.

Project Time vs. Work Time

Project managers normally track time and effort as a way to measure progress on project tasks. If you are fortunate enough to work in a fully resourced, highly disciplined environment, the time and effort you track for the project will be equivalent to the time

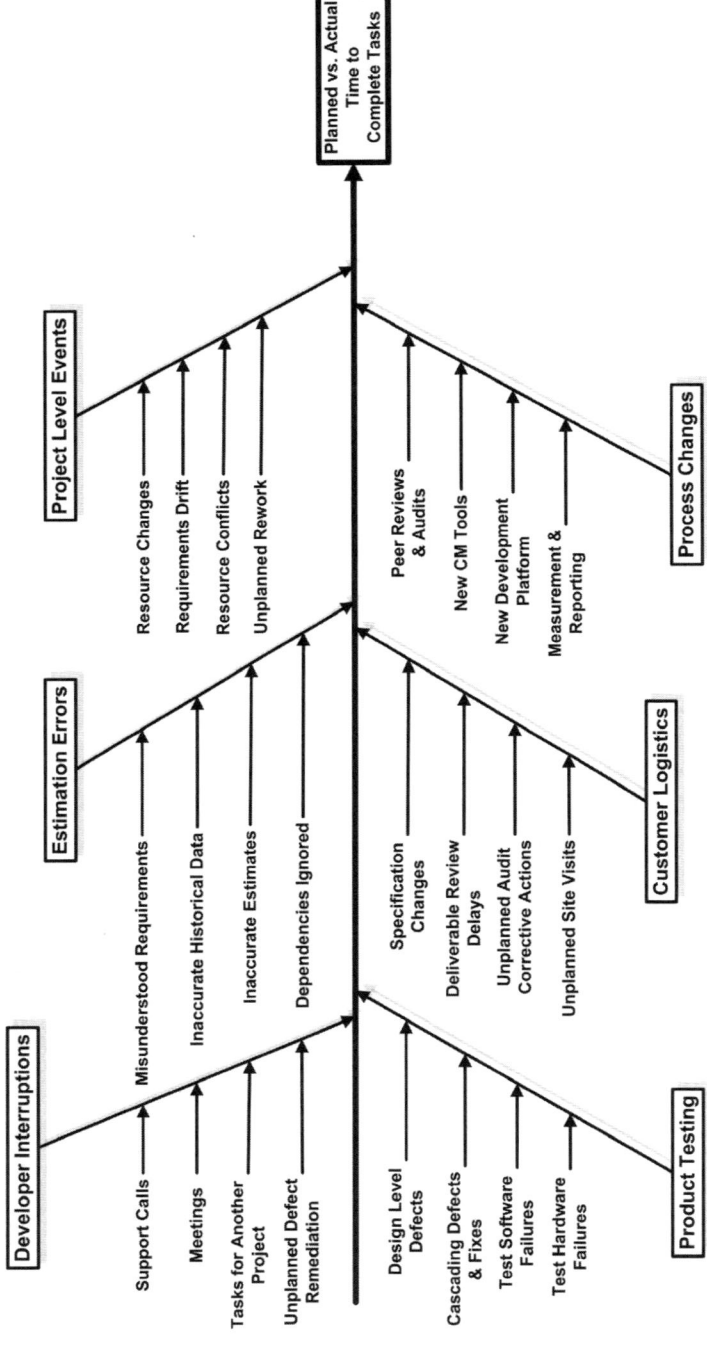

Figure 3-4 ■ Reasons for Discrepancies between Planned and Actual Time to Complete Tasks

and effort your team spends. In most environments, however, the development team is usually called upon to perform work for other departments and individuals. In these environments, there's sometimes a wide gap between the time measured in the project plan and the actual workday. Measuring this difference between "project time" and "work time" can be extremely important to your project's success.

Start by asking two questions:

1. How does your team spend its time?
2. How do you spend *your* time?

Your software and test engineers should be spending the majority of their days in requirements engineering, systems engineering, design, coding, and test preparation and execution. Are they also spending time supporting the sales force? Or the field service personnel? Are they being interrupted to help the marketing folks get the new demo set up for the next trade show? Are they spending time fixing defects from previous releases—time that is not taken into consideration on your project plan and isn't accounted for anywhere? How much time is spent per day in meetings that are not directly related to the current project?

Obviously, the less time the developers and testers are spending on the tasks at hand, the less time they will have to complete those tasks. This does not necessarily mean that they are going to be less "productive." It does mean, however, that they have less time to focus on the tasks you have assigned to them.

Where do you spend your days? On the floor working with and listening to your project team members, or in meetings haggling over release dates and content, or maybe defending the department's quality record or transfer rates? How you spend your time is a measure of the health of your organization. It's also a good indicator of what you need to measure. The crisis *du jour* for you and the engineering managers will likely become tomorrow's interruptions for the staff.

Many aspects of "work time" can be measured: meetings, support, maintenance, and the various engineering tasks. Even if your team is already accustomed to detailed time tracking for projects, your time tracking tool and your team are probably not ready for logging things like five minutes on the phone, "casual" conversations with a product manager about a future project, etc. You only have to measure what you need to know, and that may well be only direct labor and delays or interruptions.

Figure 3-5 shows the base measures you will need for time tracking, regardless of the specific aspects you choose to measure. The category of "blocked time" represents time that your project team members are prevented from working on a task because of some problem in the workflow.

Typical Time and Effort Run Rates

Run rates for time or effort are fairly straightforward. Once you have decided the measurement point, you simply chart out the estimated time or effort against the actual time or effort. In Figures 3-6 and 3-7, the measurement points used are development iterations. Each iteration is a miniature development cycle in itself. The development team establishes the requirements for that segment of the product, completes the required designs, and then codes and tests that product segment. As you can see from the effort data, the original estimates for direct labor hours were inaccurate.

Time-related Measurements	By Task	By Lifecycle Phase	By Project or Release Cycle
Estimated Time	●	●	◉
Actual Time	●	●	◉
Blocked Time	●	◉	◉
Estimated Start-to-Finish Duration in Project Plan	●	●	◉
Actual Start-to-Finish Duration in Project Plan	●	●	◉

Filled circles indicate that the measure and the measurement point are critical to your project. Partially filled circles indicate the measure and the measurement point can be used in cross-project comparisons as long as the tasks and execution environments are similar.

Figure 3-5 ● Time-related Base Measures and When to Apply Them

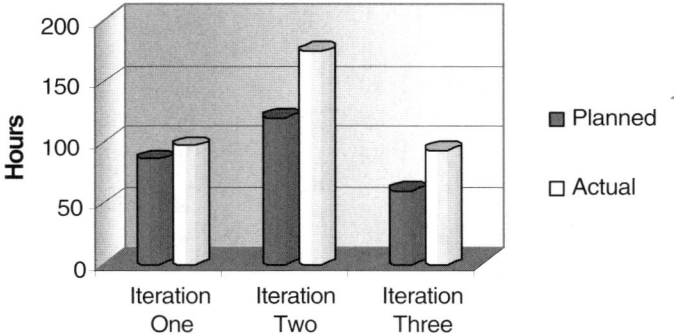

Figure 3-6 ● Planned vs. Actual Effort for Three Development Iterations

Not surprisingly, the project total effort budget was also thrown off course by the additional, unplanned hours. Figure 3-7 shows the effort for the project across the three iterations. The columns indicate the expected percent complete, in direct labor hours, at the end of each iteration.

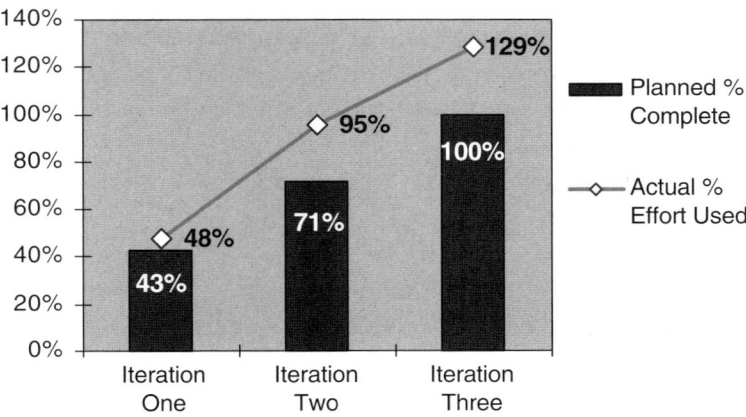

Figure 3-7 ● Planned vs. Actual Hours Expenditure for Three
Development Iterations

Had all gone as planned, it would have taken 71 percent of the project's total estimated hours to reach the end of Iteration Two. But while the actuals for Iteration One tracked close to the estimates, the actuals for Iteration Two did not. The project had already used up 95 percent of the budgeted labor hours by the time it reached the end of Iteration Two. When it finished Iteration Three, the project was 29 percent over budget for direct labor.

Like defect run rate data, time and effort run rates tell you where you are but not how you got there. A host of possible reasons may account for why the estimations for the second and third iterations were inaccurate. As a project manager, you'd want to sit down with the project team and examine all the causes for the discrepancies between the estimates and the actuals. Some of the estimates were probably off because no one really had any idea how long some tasks would take. The good news is that you now have some real data to use in the next estimation process. Some of the estimates may have been fairly accurate but "something got in the way" and the team couldn't finish some tasks on time. That's one aspect of time tracking that is often overlooked in software projects, yet it can pose your greatest risk to on-time completion.

The Hidden Danger of Blocked Time

Keep in mind that project plans assume that project tasks are more or less linear. Work breakdown structures and the critical path are the Newtonian physics of project management: billiard balls hitting other billiard balls and causing predictable and expected behavior. Thanks to research in psychosocial nonlinear dynamics, we now know that organizational behavior in general and project-level behavior in particular are far more unpredictable and far less structured than we thought. Nonetheless, in that linear project management world, either you are making forward progress toward the end date or you are not. That makes time measurements a little easier to design.

If the goal is 100 percent utilization of all planned time, then the measure only has to distinguish between productive time and unproductive time. Productive time is planned time for planned tasks, unplanned time for planned tasks, and planned and unplanned time in rework for the current project or release. Unproductive time is time spent waiting on resources, waiting on information, or performing other tasks that have interrupted the current project (such as maintenance for a previous release).

"Unproductive" has negative connotations in business, so you'll need to use a different term for this category of time. "Blocked" carries the sense of forward movement stalled by something or someone. When the development team can't make progress on a specification because they are waiting on information from someone in Sales, they are blocked. When the test team can't make progress on a test suite because their test hardware failed, they are blocked.

Blocked time often goes unnoticed when the main focus is on meeting dates, and it is hard to track with a time-tracking utility. This kind of information is so useful in highlighting the real costs of inefficiencies in your department and across departments, however, that it's worth a little extra effort to collect the data. Have the team members keep a time-tracking sheet. Figure 3-8 shows a sample timesheet that combines task types, project dates, and detailed time tracking.

Task	Project Plan Start Date	Project Plan Finish Date	Project Estimated Duration	Actual Duration	Blocked Time
Test Prep	3/17/2004	4/12/2004	8	8	0
Regression	3/22/2004	3/24/2004			
Component 1	3/22/2004	3/23/2004	11	6	3
Component 2	3/22/2004	3/23/2004	9	6	
TC Development	3/17/2004	4/12/2004			
Feature A	3/23/2004	3/26/2004	24	24	10
Feature B	3/24/2004	3/29/2004	12	12	
Feature C	3/29/2004	4/19/2004	20	20	
Initial Testing	3/29/2004	4/6/2004			
Feature A	4/2/2004	4/12/2004	32	32	40
Feature B	3/30/2004	4/1/2004	16	16	4
Feature C	4/2/2004	4/8/2004	40	24	

Figure 3-8 ● Estimated Labor Time, Actual Time, and Blocked Time

To limit the initial overhead, select whatever task types are most important to your needs, keeping in mind that what meets your staff's needs will probably meet yours as well. For example, both you and your development managers can benefit from knowing how long it takes to diagnose and fix problems reported from test and reported from the field. You and your test managers will want to know the relative percentage of time used to create test plans and test cases versus the time spent executing the tests.

Over time, this information also supports more accurate resource and duration estimations in the planning stages of a project. For example, the data in Figure 3-9 should prompt you to add some contingency time to future schedules for at least the initial testing phase to cover the blocked time. Finally, when coupled with defect trending data, this information can be used to estimate the risk to project resource plans and schedules for support and maintenance (or even to build that into the resource plan).

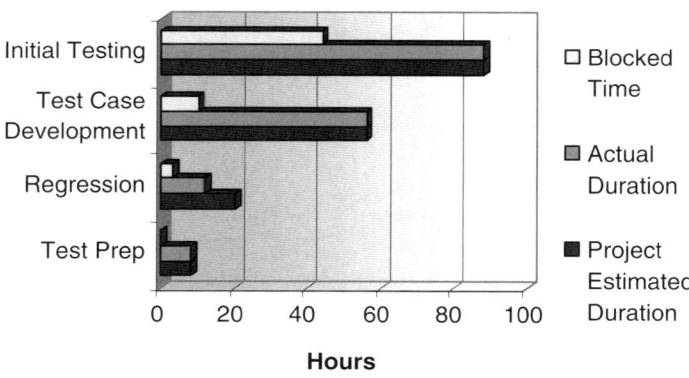

Figure 3-9 ● Sample Time Utilization Chart

● APPLYING WHAT YOU'VE LEARNED

We have discussed many factors that can cause peaks or troughs in run rate data. The following exercises will give you a chance to use that information to interpret run rate data.

Exercise 3-1: Interpreting Defect Run Rates

Each of the exercises below presents you with a graph of defect run rate data and asks you questions about the significance of the data. These are thought questions; there's no right or wrong answer. If you don't feel you have enough information to adequately answer the question, think about what additional information you would like to have. One of the goals of these exercises is to help you understand the limitations of run rate data.

Exercise 3-1a:

Consider the defect discovery data in Figure 3-10. Without any other information about the development project, what can you reasonably conclude from the chart?

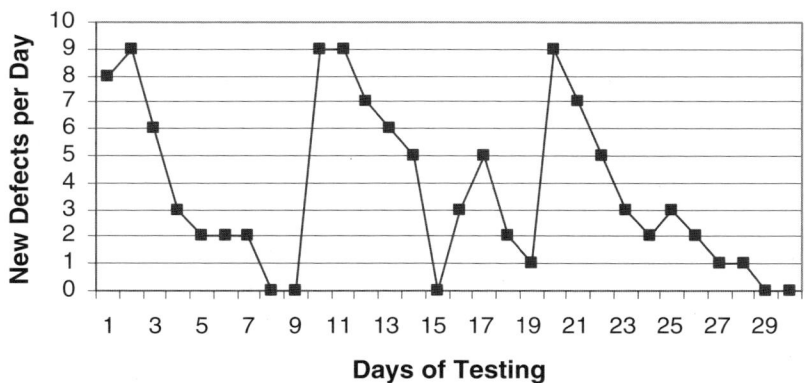

Figure 3-10 ● Data for Exercise 3-1a

Now let us add some background information. The test cycle is 30 days long, with builds delivered to the test team on days 1, 10, and 20. Based on what you've learned in this chapter, answer the following questions:

1. What are reasonable explanations for the peaks in the data?
2. What information do you need to understand the reason for the peak around days 16 and 17?

3. Is the product ready to ship on day 31? If not, what other information would you need to help you make that decision?

Exercise 3-1b:

Suppose we have the same product, same development and test team, and same schedule as in the first exercise. In this case, however, the defect run rate is slightly different, as shown in Figure 3-11.

1. How are the charts similar and dissimilar?
2. Are there similar peaks and troughs?
3. What might cause the similarity in the peaks? What would cause the change in the timing of those peaks?
4. Would you say the product can ship on day 31? Why or why not?

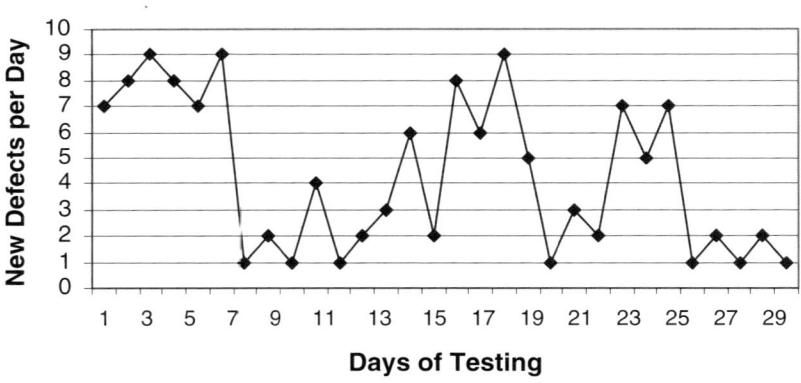

Figure 3-11 ● Data for Exercise 3-1b

Exercise 3-1c:

This time, suppose you are completing your first project in a development organization that has kept run rate data for two previous projects. The data displayed in the charts for the previous two exercises represents the run rate data for the previous two projects. Both

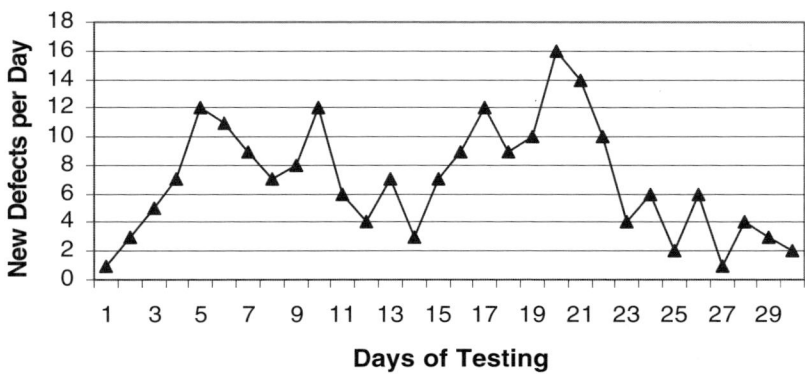

Figure 3-12 ● Data for Exercise 3-1c

of those projects involved the same product you are working on. The teams were the same and the schedules were almost identical.

Figure 3-12 contains your run rate data.

Using the charts from the previous two projects (Figures 3-10 and 3-11 in the previous two exercises), answer the following questions:

1. What can you tell about your project and your readiness to ship?
2. What other information would you want to have to help you understand the similarities and dissimilarities between your run rates and those of your predecessors?

CHAPTER

4

Behind the Lines:
Attribute Analyses

You sit back in your chair and breathe a sigh of relief. You've just received an email from the build master announcing the start of the build for the test team. Yesterday you weren't sure you'd make the testing milestone on time. When the development team found two new defects in the communications module late in the afternoon, no one knew how severe the problems were. But the developers worked into the night and fixed both bugs, and the development team is going out for beer and pizza to celebrate a job well done. You're thinking you might join them—after all, your project is back on schedule.

But for how long?

Project milestones are a somewhat arbitrary measure of completion in any project, but they can be particularly misleading in software development projects. The tasks that went into completing a particular development phase may well have ended on the due date specified in the project plan. The results of those tasks won't be known for some time, however. From requirements specification, through design, and on to code completion, many people take many actions—every one of which may affect the project later on. In a software project, attaining a milestone and being on schedule can be quite different things.

To assess the real impact to the project schedule of these eleventh-hour fixes, you would need answers to questions such as:

- ➡ Were the problems fully analyzed?
- ➡ Were the proposed code changes fully reviewed before they were implemented?
- ➡ Was the unit testing of the changed code focused only on success paths or did the developers test all possible inputs, outputs, and error conditions?
- ➡ What other functions in the product might be affected by these changes?
- ➡ Will the test team be able to test these possible side effects?
- ➡ Do they have time to test for these side effects under the current schedule?

So how do you know whether the project is on schedule? If you had both the time and the expertise, you could review the design documents, the change specifications, the affected code, the test cases, etc. But most software project managers can't spend several hours reviewing every defect. Nor do they usually possess the software engineering background necessary to critically analyze each and every change across the entire product. The software measures discussed in this chapter will give you insight into the quality and risks in the work completed to date, as well as let you assess any further risks to your project.

● KEY DEFECT ATTRIBUTES

A project manager requires different information from a problem report than a developer or tester does. The developer wants to know what operations trigger the defect and what the failure symptoms are. The tester wants to see if the code change fixed the problem. The project manager, on the other hand, wants to know what implications the defect holds for the project's schedule or resource allocations. From the project management perspective, the following defect attributes are most interesting:

- *Status*—where the problem report is in the workflow of finding and fixing defects
- *Injection phase*—the project task, activity, or phase in which the defect was introduced
- *Detection phase*—the project task, activity, or phase in which the defect was discovered.

Unlike run rate data, which doesn't help you understand the reasons why the line graphs look as they do, attribute analysis helps you understand the role of the development processes behind the data. For example:

➡ Is the team successfully managing its development and maintenance cycles?

➡ What aspect(s) of the project contribute to the defect discovery-and-repair cycle?

➡ What project tasks are detecting defects, or is the customer doing the project's testing for it?

Taking measurements of these three attributes at different times in the lifecycle and combining the measurements in different ways is a powerful tool for seeing past the bug of the day to more subtle development process issues as well as more pervasive product quality issues. The different attributes provide different perspectives on your project: status is related to productivity; the injection phase is related to development process; and the detection phase is a way to measure your quality control.

● DEFECT STATUS AND PRODUCTIVITY

Like the number of defects per time period, the number of defects by status is also an incident measure. Because it focuses on state-related attributes, however, the number of defects by status can be far more informative than a measurement of the number of defects alone. Typically, the status attributes are derived from the problem reporting tool, and the status values represent the states of the report and/or the defect in the corrective action workflow. Regardless of how the states are labeled, they can give you important insight into what lies ahead in your project, even if at this moment you are on schedule.

Different defect status values have different implications for your project. A high number of "open reports" means your project team will be faced with maintenance work, which can be both time-consuming and risky. On the other hand, a high number of "closed reports" generally means that the testing and maintenance processes have been working efficiently. High incidences of the wrong type of state, at the wrong time, can be used heuristically to identify process breakdowns or future risks. What these states are and what constitutes a "wrong type" will be based on what process flow you use for development and how easy it is to extract this state data from your tracking tool.

Example: Defect Rates and States

For the example in Figures 4-1 and 4-2, assume that the problem reporting system allows reports to be in one of three states:

- New (entered but not fixed)
- Fixed
- Closed (retested successfully).

The chart in Figure 4-1 shows the weekly totals of new defects for a four-week period. Looking at this data alone, one could rea-

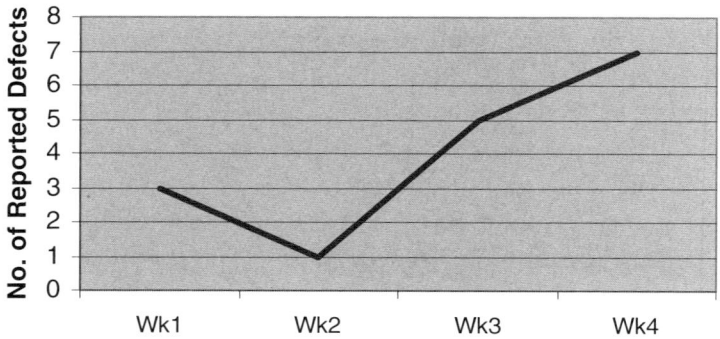

Figure 4-1 ● New Defect Rate

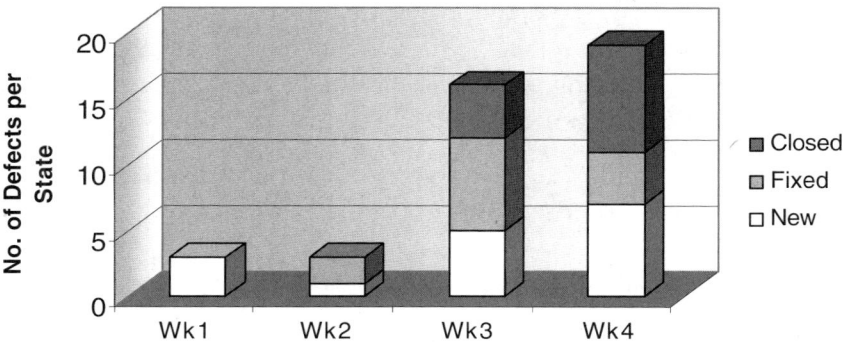

Figure 4-2 ● Defects by Status, by Week

sonably conclude that the project has a quality problem. The total number of defects has been increasing steadily for three weeks.

The situation doesn't look quite so bleak once you analyze the data in Figure 4-1 into states. The chart in Figure 4-2 shows the weekly totals over a four-week period for each possible state. The development team made good progress toward fixing and closing defect reports in Weeks 3 and 4. All is not well with this release, of course: you will want to know why the new rate is rising. Using the status attributes, you have enough information to ask other questions as well—questions that might help you understand the entire problem, not just the incidence of new reports:

➡ Why were there no defects fixed in Week 1? Were fixes delayed until Week 2 for some reason?

➡ Why are so few defects fixed in Week 2 compared with Week 3?

➡ Why does it take until Week 3 to start closing the defect reports?

➡ Do the answers to these questions point to a technical problem with the product? For example, is it difficult to fix the code because it lacks a clean design?

➜ Do the answers to these questions point to problems in the development process? For example, do the delays indicate a need to streamline the handling of defect reports and new builds between the test team and the developers?

Incidence data is valuable if it prompts you to ask questions that will improve your product and process.

● INJECTION PHASE AND THE DEVELOPMENT PROCESS

Defects can be introduced for a variety of reasons, at various times in the lifecycle, and during the execution of different tasks. They are generally discovered either during that task or in some later product evaluation activity such as a peer review or testing. The number of defects by injection phase is a diagnostic measure. It reveals where the defects originated from a process or lifecycle perspective; knowing this helps you identify deficiencies in development processes.

Too often, defects are considered to be minor problems if they have little or no impact on the performance of the product. This view may help a development team ship on time, but it may also merely postpone problems until it's risky and costly to fix them. Some defects, such as cosmetic issues with a user interface, may safely be neglected. Defects that reflect or cause deficiencies in the development *process*, however, should never be considered minor problems. It may seem like wasted effort to bring a design document up to date or to enforce code-commenting standards. Yet, these simple activities can save you time and money later on. Five minutes spent updating a document or module header now can save hours of confusion and rework in a future project phase.

Careful selection of the injection phase categories can help you distinguish defects that must be fixed from those whose fixes can be postponed. The injection phase can also help you distinguish between product defects and process deficiencies. Select those areas of the development process where there's a potential for introducing defects in both the product and the process. (A project team exercise at the end of this chapter will help you identify these areas.)

Resist the temptation to oversimplify the categories. Most defects and process failures have many possible causes, and a list that seems too detailed or cumbersome now may be precisely the tool you need in an actual release cycle. Remember too that not all software defects are code defects. A coding blunder may be traceable to a problem with the design document. Perhaps the design was incorrect. Perhaps the developer used an earlier version of the design document that had errors in it. In the first case, the defect was injected in the design process itself and the design review process failed to catch the bug. This is a process defect. On the other hand, the second case is a configuration management problem rather than a design problem, and the configuration management process needs fixing along with the code.

Example: The Significance of Injection Rates

For the example in Figure 4-3, only three possible injection phases are measured: requirements, design, and code.

- A defect with requirements as its injection phase is due to some error that occurred in collecting, analyzing, or documenting a product requirement.

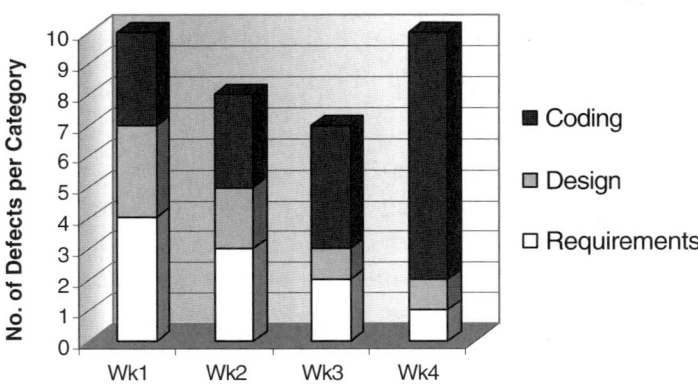

Figure 4-3 ● Example of Injection Phase Data

- Assignment to the design injection phase indicates an error in the technical aspects of the design or an error in the documentation of that design.
- Coding defects are programming language-level or algorithmic defects not caused by deficiencies in requirements or design.

The injection phase is a diagnostic measure because it tells you something about the cause for the defects. In the example in Figure 4-3, the total number of defects per week during the four-week period initially drops and then peaks in Week 4. Once again, though, there's more to the story than just the number of defects. The rates of requirements-related defects and design-related defects decrease during the four-week period. This indicates that, despite the defect incidence rates, the testing effort is clearing the product of requirements-related and design-related defects. In effect, there is good news behind the bad news.

Even a diagnostic measure such as injection phase is limited in what it can tell you about your product and processes, however. Like defect status data, it should prompt you to probe behind the numbers to what's going on in the development process:

→ Why do the coding defect rates spike in Week 4?
→ Does this spike indicate a change in test approach?
→ Does the spike indicate that testing started covering a part of the product that was poorly coded?
→ Does the spike indicate that testing started exercising a part of the product that hadn't been tested recently, and these are legacy defects just now coming to light?

Always treat measurement data as an invitation to look behind the spreadsheet to the planning and execution of software development tasks. Every product defect represents either a deficiency in the processes used to produce the product or an inefficiency in the processes used to produce the product. Under the pressure to ship on time, defects are often looked upon as annoying, costly mistakes. Don't forget that they also represent opportunities.

● DETECTION PHASE AND QUALITY CONTROL

The number of defects by detection phase is a diagnostic measure. Typically, detection points are the places where the product is evaluated, such as reviews of specifications or code, internal testing, beta test or customer acceptance testing, and post-release. Since this measure reveals where the defects were discovered, the data can help you identify deficiencies in quality control-related development processes. This measure typically is used to:

- Benchmark your current detection locations and rates in advance of process changes.
- Determine if process changes have improved your ability to catch defects earlier by comparing current detection rates with previous rates for the same detection points.
- Establish the detection rates for cost-of-quality calculations, either to show current costs of poor quality or the cost reductions from process changes. (Costs are addressed in Chapter 5.)

Example: The Ones That Got Away

Figure 4-4 compares the detection phase data for three releases. Most of the defects in Release A and Release B were found during the test cycle. Release C, on the other hand, has a higher detection rate in the requirements review and a lower detection rate in code and test than do Release A and Release B. The data seems to reinforce a common assumption in software quality assurance: the more defects discovered early in the cycle, the fewer that will be discovered late in the cycle.

To take another example, the example in Figure 4-5 illustrates detection phase data for two releases. For Release X, more defects were discovered in peer reviews than by testers or the customer. This is good news about the quality of the product, and it is even better news if you accept the software industry's maxim that the earlier a defect is detected, the less it costs to fix it.

On the other hand, Release Y's data is troubling. Peer reviews were conducted, but the reviews found fewer defects than did the

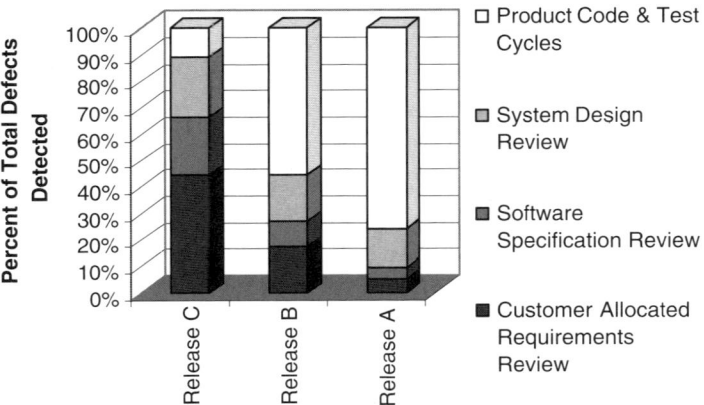

Figure 4-4 ● Detection Rates

testers or the customer. We would want to look into the possible reasons for this unusual "detection profile," such as:

➤ Were peer reviews held for all changes to the product or just for some changes?
➤ Does the test detection data come from the areas that were not peer-reviewed?

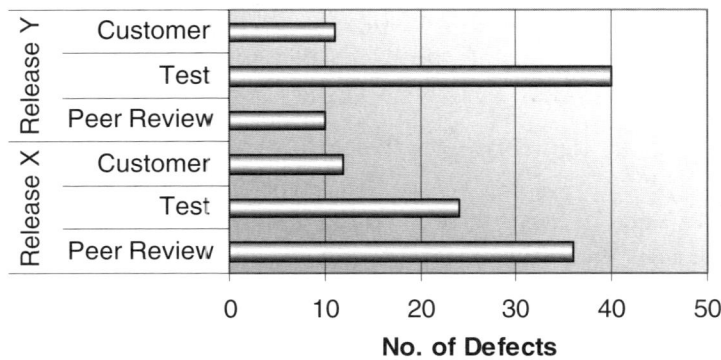

Figure 4-5 ● Example of Detection Phase Data

➡ Does the peer review process need to be made more robust?

➡ Does the current process need to be enforced better?

➡ Does the detection data indicate a wider scope in testing than was used in the reviews? (For example, reviews are not as good at detecting performance problems as stress testing is.)

➡ Does the test detection data include unit test data as well as integration or systems testing data? Could that account for the comparatively high detection rate?

➡ What kinds of problems did the customer find that escaped both reviews and testing?

● KEY TIME AND EFFORT ATTRIBUTES

Your development team has a fairly limited view of time utilization: they work on a task and complete a timesheet. You, on the other hand, need to monitor time utilization by both individual tasks and by task types. As you plan out your project tasks, think about the time and effort attributes you will want to measure: blocked time, effort per development "phase" or category of activity, etc.

Typically, the key time and effort attributes will include many or all of the following items. Time is assumed to be the duration of the activity (planned and actual), and effort is the amount of direct labor hours of one or more individuals (planned and actual).

- Time/effort spent in requirements generation and specification.
- Time/effort spent in design and design documentation.
- Time/effort spent coding and unit testing. (If, in your environment, unit testing is a separate activity from coding and is performed by someone other than the developer, separate unit testing from coding.)
- Time/effort spent in preparation for testing: research, test case development, etc.
- Time/effort spent in testing for the planned test cycle(s).
- Time/effort spent in defect analysis and correction (rework).
- Time/effort spent in retesting corrected defects (rework).
- Blocked time in any category above.

- Time/effort spent in any defect prevention activity, such as requirements reviews, design reviews, or code reviews.

This is a long list, especially if your project team is not used to recording their hours. But the finer the granularity of the time and effort data, the more useful it is. In fact, when you combine the defect-related attributes with detailed time- or effort-related attributes, you can diagnose problems down to the software-component level.

● PUTTING THE PIECES TOGETHER: ITERATIVE DEVELOPMENT RISK ANALYSIS

It's time to show how the various measures discussed so far can be combined to help you understand what's really happening in your project. For this extended illustration, we'll assume that the key effort attributes are effort required for requirements, for design, for code, and for test.

At the end of Chapter 3 we briefly looked at the data from an ill-fated iterative development project. That project ended 29 percent over its budget for effort, due in part to a significant and unexpected increase in effort in the second iteration (see Figure 4-6).

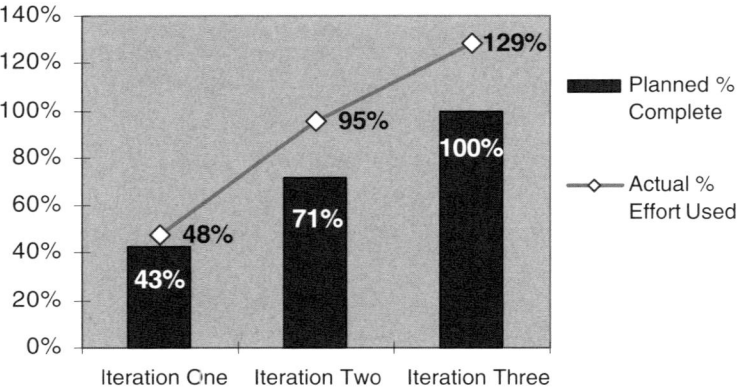

Figure 4-6 ● Overrun in an Iterative Development Project

By the end of Iteration Two, the effort rates alone would have alerted any project manager to serious risks in the project. But there's no information here to indicate what kind of risks the project faces going forward. As a result, there's no way to know how to mitigate those risks. This is where attribute data can be useful.

Assume for the sake of illustration that the product comprises four components, Comp1 through Comp4. The iterative strategy used in the project calls for two development cycles and an integration cycle.

In the first iteration, the goal is to develop the first two components and have them evaluated by the customer. The second iteration includes the development of two more components and the interfaces to the previous two. That iteration also ends with a customer evaluation period of the individual components.

To simplify integration testing, the components are integrated and tested in two stages in the third iteration:

- In the first stage, Comp1, Comp2, and Comp3 are integrated and tested.
- In the second stage, Comp4 is integrated with Comp1, Comp2, and Comp3 and tested.

The iteration ends with a final customer acceptance test.

The effort for the first two iterations is shown in Figures 4-7 and 4-8. In the first iteration (Figure 4-7), Comp1 and Comp2 were tracking close to expectations for requirements generation, design and code, and customer evaluation testing. During the second iteration (Figure 4-8), Comp4 tracked close to expectations, but Comp3 did not. Comp3 exceeded planned hours in all categories: requirements generation, design and code, and evaluation. It is tempting to look at the spikes in requirements generation and evaluation as the cause of the project overrun. However, these are really just symptoms of the actual problems.

Looking at the defect rates for the components at the end of the second iteration in Figure 4-9, we find that Comp3 has the most defects. We might have expected that, based on the extra time it took

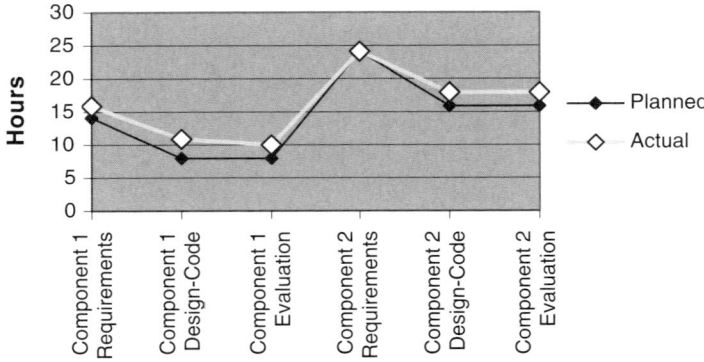

Figure 4-7 ■ Effort for Iteration One

to evaluate the component. Is Comp3 the only component we have to worry about? Probably not.

Figure 4-9 also shows a high defect discovery total for Comp2 and Comp4. This should set off alarms on any project manager's desktop. Three components are showing high defect rates but only one of them is showing any other symptoms of product or process problems. What's hiding under the defect data? What are the implications for the third iteration?

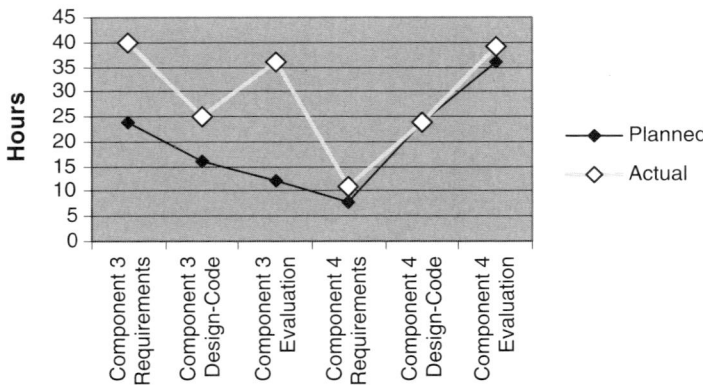

Figure 4-8 ■ Effort for Iteration Two

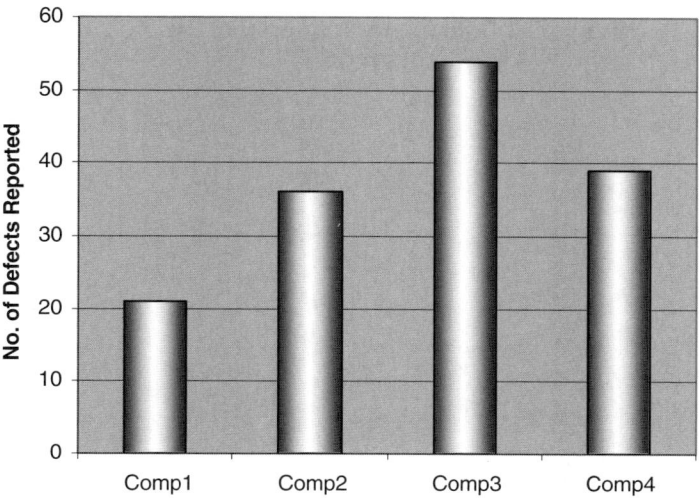

Figure 4-9 ■ Component Defect Totals at the End of Iteration Two

To find out what's hiding in the defect data, we need to look at the attributes of injection phase and detection phase. This data is shown in Figures 4-10 and 4-11. Keeping in mind that this is iterative development, we expect to see a fair number of defects introduced in the requirements phase, since the iteration as a whole is, in a way, one long requirements management effort. Similarly, we expect to find that the majority of defects are detected in the evaluation phase, where the customer has the chance to see the product in action and provide input. In these figures, it is not the actual number that matters as much as the comparison across components.

The first thing you should notice in the injection phase data is the trend toward increasing number of defects. There were more requirements-related defects in Comp4 than in Comp3, more design-related problems in Comp2 than in Comp1, and so forth. This is a cause for concern because the components so far have only been tested individually. It won't be until Iteration Three that the components will be integrated and retested.

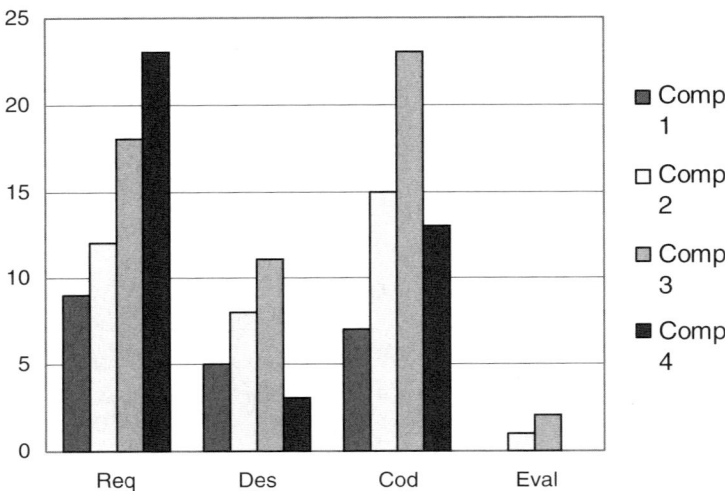

Figure 4-10 ● Component Injection Phase Data

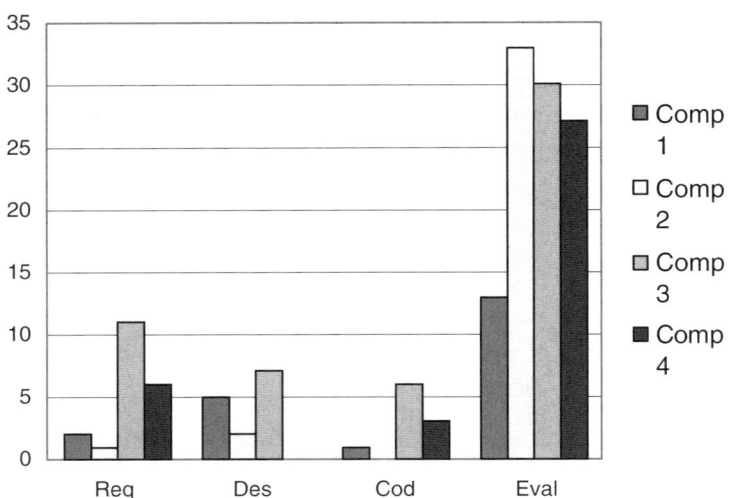

Figure 4-11 ● Component Detection Phase Data

To complete this analysis, let's look at where the defects are being found. For example, if the majority of requirements-related defects are being caught in the requirements reviews, a high defect incidence won't have as damaging an effect on the project as it might if all defects were being caught in the evaluation phase.

Unfortunately, the detection phase data shows just the opposite. The majority of defects are being detected in the evaluation or test phase. Worse, Comp3 has the best early detection rate, yet it remains the most obviously problematic of the components.

Suppose for a moment that you are the project manager for this development project. At the end of Iteration Two, you know your project is in trouble: you've almost used up your budgeted hours. If you didn't have this data, what would you likely have done? You would probably have seen it as a resource issue. You would probably have asked the team to work untracked overtime or spent some of your contingency fund to get an extra resource to get the project back on track.

But now that you've seen the data, what should you do?

It should be clear that this isn't just a headcount issue. One component of the product has obvious quality problems, and there's evidence to suggest that two other components may be defect-prone. A significant portion of the testing has yet to be performed, so the risk remains high. Adding a tester might speed up the test time. If the product is buggy, then that additional tester will just generate more work for the developers. As a result, any progress you make in testing might come at the cost of slowing down the final development tasks.

The solution has less to do with resources than it does with tactics. As you may recall, the original iteration plan calls for integrating and testing Comp4 in the second stage of the third iteration cycle. Since Comp4 may be defect-prone, it doesn't make sense to test it late in the iteration. Recall also that the plan calls for a final customer acceptance test after the two stages have been completed. Given that Comp4 had a higher rate of requirements-related defects than

Comp3, it might be prudent to involve the customer in the integration testing instead of waiting for their input at acceptance time.

This would be a good time to close the spreadsheet program, walk down to the developer cubicles, and talk over changing the test approaches. While you are there, you should get their input on Comp2, Comp3, and Comp4:

→ What kinds of requirements-related problems did they encounter for the components?

→ Are there any similarities between Comp3 and Comp4 that the test team can use to get to the critical defects in Comp4 more quickly?

→ Comp2 had a high number of defects found in test. What kinds of defects did they find in Comp2?

→ Are there any similarities between Comp2 and Comp4 that could be exploited in testing to get out the defects more quickly?

→ How might the recent bug fixes to Comp3 have affected the interfaces between components? Can the developers think of any fixes that might have adversely affected Comp4?

There's never a silver bullet lying around when you need one, and a project that is at 95 percent of budgeted hours with a third of the project to go will never make the CFO's Top 10 Favorite Projects list. Nonetheless, it should be clear at this point that even if your software measures don't fully explain the nature of the problem, they will at least help you ask the appropriate questions and take appropriate corrective action.

● PROBLEM REPORT TRACKING SYSTEM REQUIREMENTS

I hope that by now you've started to appreciate how powerful a tool these simple measures can be. You are probably wondering how you can obtain this variety of data. The good news is that the measures discussed in this chapter are easily tracked with any of the commercial project, time tracking, and problem reporting packages available today. The not-so-good news is that most of the problem tracking packages will require some customization to meet all the base measure needs described so far. There are certain generic requirements for a tracking system, regardless of which package you actually use.

Your problem tracking system must support four basic functions:

- Report and defect management
- Impact assessment
- Effort assessment
- Development process evaluation.

The categories and the specific information required in each function are shown in Figure 4-12. (To simplify the discussion, the typical descriptive sections, such as expected and actual results or steps to reproduce, are omitted here.)

The functions are fairly straightforward. Given a problem report, you need to know:

- *Configuration information*—the platform and versions of hardware or software where the problem arose, and where the problem was fixed.
- *Impact information*—the impact that the problem has on the customer and the impact that the fix will have on the development organization.
- *Effort information*—the time already expended on the defect, the time to fix it, and the time to retest the fix.
- *Process performance information*—what the problem implies about how well the development process is working with respect to product quality.

In the ideal system, information for each category would be captured in separate fields, such as "time to fix" or "effect of change." Each of these fields should present a standard set of values to select from. For the text fields, you should be able to select more than one value in each field. For the time fields, it is typically easiest to supply some range of values to pick from: .5, 1.0, 1.5, 2.0 hours, etc. Although these values for the time fields will not give you a precise accounting of the time, they will simplify logging the time.

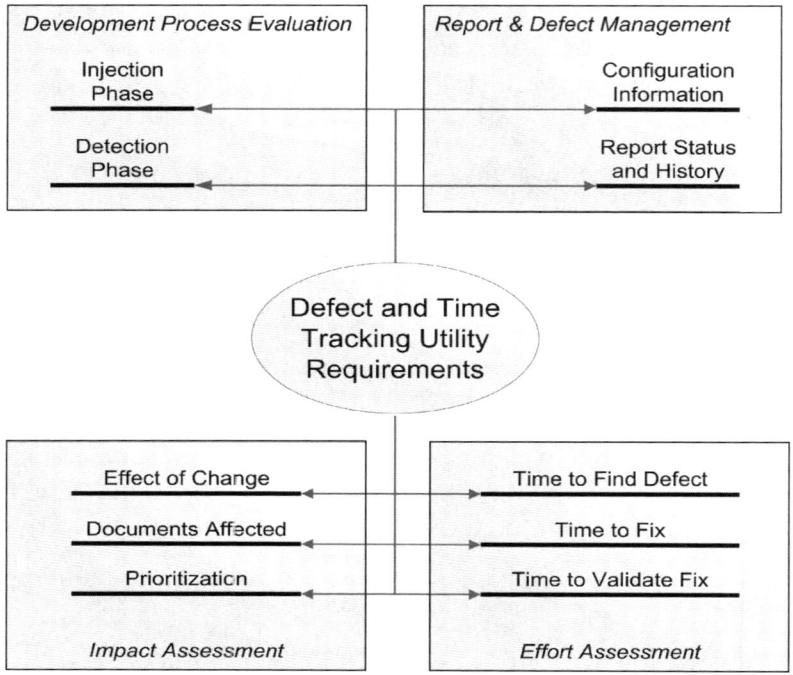

Figure 4-12 ■ Requirements for Tracking Defects and Time

The values for the fields are a matter of your information needs and your development culture. A sample set is discussed below.

Injection Phase

The values in this field categorize your development lifecycle into phases or groups of tasks that can introduce defects into the product. These categories typically include:

- Requirements generation (product or customer requirements, system requirements, software requirements, and statutory or safety requirements)

- Design (high-level, low-level)
- Coding (prototyping, final coding, unit testing)
- Test development (use case development, test case development, test software development)
- Planning (inadequate time allocated, inadequate resources allocated)
- Configuration management (configuration item not uniquely identified, configuration impact of change not identified, build errors, version compatibility errors).

Detection Phase

Use this field to identify project events, milestones, or interfaces where defects can be detected. These typically include:

- Requirements specification or review (as above)
- Design specification or review (as above)
- Coding (defects can be discovered in another's code while coding)
- Internal testing
- External testing (Beta testing, field testing, acceptance testing)
- Initial warranty period
- Maintenance.

Note that the detection phase generally has to be a project phase to support phase containment.

Effect of Change

Values in this field are a way to manage the "housekeeping" associated with a fix. Too often code fixes are looked at in isolation from any associated documents or procedures, so this field should have values for whatever work products and processes can be affected by a code change. These values signal other groups or individuals that their documents or procedures may require modification.

Review the product's problem reports and categorize the kinds of changes that are made in answer to the problem reports. These typically include new configuration requirement, new installation requirement, training documentation change, software documentation change, user interface change, feature enhancement, embedded function correction, and embedded function enhancement.

Documentation Affected

Similar to effect of change, this field specifies which documents must be changed after a fix. These field values could be mingled with the effect of change values, or this field could include only those documents that the development organization maintains.

Identify the types of documentation the team produces. Typical field values might be installation instructions, user manuals, training materials, requirements documents, design documents, release notes, online help, and online support or advisory documents.

Prioritization

The priority category can be approached in two ways. This field typically reflects the relative importance of the problem. If you take this approach to priority, you must first determine how you want to define importance. Does it reflect how quickly the customer wants the fix? How quickly they really need it? Or does it reflect how quickly the development team needs to address the problem?

On the other hand, several defect attributes can be combined as a way of defining priority. This approach might subdivide priority into customer-perceived severity, frequency of problem occurrence, penetration of the defect in the installed base, likelihood of defect occurring, and risk of the change. (See Appendix B for an example of this approach to priority.)

Configuration Information

Most problem tracking systems will allow you to record the software version or hardware version where the problem appeared. Ideally, however, the problem report should include all the relevant system configuration information in case it is needed for problem diagnosis. This level of detail is also useful in identifying compatibility issues and in finding inconsistencies in a customer's configuration.

The configuration information for the fix must include the version that contains the fix. If defects can be put on hold and assigned into a future release, the tracking tool should identify that release. The configuration information must also identify the source files that were changed. This helps ensure that all the affected files are built. It also helps test personnel determine the full impact of a change and identify what, if anything, needs to be tested beyond the operational sequence where the defect was first discovered.

Report Status and History

Status is the key piece of information used in defect run rates and Change Control Board activity. The state labels can be whatever makes sense in your environment, as long as the values will help you track a defect's state and determine the workload for the Change Control Board, development, and test.

Deferral rates can be tracked here or in the configuration information. If the problem report tool allows the Change Control Board to assign a defect into a future release, then you will be able to track deferred reports on the basis of their assigned version. If the tool does not provide this capability, then the state of "deferred" should be added to the status field values.

Defect/Fix Status

If process defects and problem reports need to be reported separately (such as when the customer outage report system is separate from the internal defect reporting system), the problem report tracking system will need to identify the status of the defect or fix.

Time Fields

Time fields can include time to find the defect during test, time to fix it, and time to retest the affected area of the product. It is helpful in advanced measurement to have the planned and actuals recorded.

● SHOULD YOU MEASURE DEFECT "SEVERITY" RATINGS?

Defect significance (often called severity, criticality, or priority) is a problematic concept. Two measures of status are commonly tracked: the severity of the defect and the priority of the defect. Severity is usually defined in terms of its impact on the customer or the product. Priority can be defined either as how urgently the customer needs the fix from development or the priority of the fix among all the other defects the development team has to fix.

Severity and priority are usually given hierarchical values, such as "showstopper," high, medium, and low. Priority can be measured using some classification scheme that helps the development team schedule the fix in its total workload, such as critical, urgent, high, and low. These units of measurement have some drawbacks. First, they obviously have a subjective component. A showstopper to one customer may be a low to another. Second, the qualitative aspect of the units means they can be more easily manipulated than purely quantitative values. Does a showstopper have to be fixed by the next build or only by shipment? What prevents development from downgrading a set of defect reports to get those reports off their plate a week before the planned ship date?

If you are going to measure severity and priority of defects and use that information either in product quality assessments or in rework planning, you need to make sure that the data is consistent. Many organizations use matrices (see Figures 4-13 and 4-14) to define the values and to identify which combinations are legitimate.

If this approach to determining defect significance is used, data collection and display are simply a variation on raw defect incidence. The number of defects is determined by status at whatever milestones seem appropriate. Since this kind of status is so subjective, it is obviously heuristic and it is not very useful as an indicator. If the problem severity is supplied by the customers, you can at least get a sense of how the customers see your product defects over time. Priority is simply too imprecise a measure to support meaningful comparisons over time, however.

Severity Value	Definition	Priority Value	Definition
Showstopper	System down. No operations can complete.	Critical	Must be fixed and a special build must be scheduled so a patch can be released to customer.
High	Single user is prevented from completing tasks.	Urgent	Must be fixed in the next regularly scheduled build. No patch required.
Medium	System performance is slow.	High	Must be fixed in the next release cycle.
Low	Customer finds function annoying.	Low	May be postponed until some future release.

Figure 4-13 ● Sample Value Definitions for Severity and Priority

	Critical	Urgent	High	Low
Showstopper	X	X		
High		X	X	
Medium			X	X
Low				X

Figure 4-14 ● Sample Matrix for Admissible Combinations of Values

Given the limitations on the severity and priority measures, it is best not to use them at all in derived measures or indicators. If your problem tracking tool will support the necessary modifications, you're better off replacing severity and priority with an orthogonal defect classification scheme or with the alternative discussed in Appendix B.

● APPLYING WHAT YOU'VE LEARNED

These exercises will give you some experience in interpreting defect rates, injection and detection phases, and in performing risk analysis using defects and time.

Exercise 4-1: Looking into the Future

Since we looked at *defect* status earlier, let's use *problem report* status in a derived measure—in this case, the deferred state for problem reports. There's always pressure to remove problem reports from the current release and defer them to a future release. This does more than simply postpone a specific defect fix; it adds work to the next release effort, sapping resources and time from the next project. If you are the project manager for a product line, you will want to ensure that the development team or Change Control Board is not overburdening the project you haven't even kicked off yet!

Figure 4-15 shows the backlog of problem reports assigned to be fixed in future releases and the release in which they originated.

The development team has assigned a large number of defects found in the current release into the next future release, Future Release 1. The team has also assigned some current defects into two more future releases, Future Releases 2 and 3. This seems to be a standard procedure for this team. All future releases include a legacy of defects from previous Releases A and B as well. While it would be hasty to draw any conclusions from this chart alone, it would be prudent to ask several questions to determine the risks involved with this practice of deferring defects. Two relevant questions are:

→ Are we deferring defects that will cause significant loss of customer satisfaction while they wait for the fix?
→ Have we assigned so many legacy defects into the future releases that there's no time in the schedule for fixing new defects found in the code being introduced in those releases?

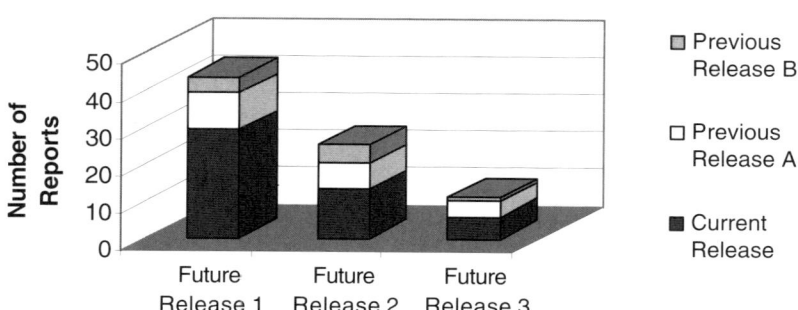

Figure 4-15 ● Problem Report Backlog Assignments

What other questions would you need answered to determine the risks involved in the deferral rate?

Exercise 4-2: Interpreting Detection Phase Data

This exercise asks you to extrapolate from previous release data to your current development effort.

You have been assigned as project manager for Version 2.0 of the OopsTryThis software application. Version 1.0 was developed and released by Project A.

Exercise 4-2a

The detection phase data for that project cycle is shown in Figure 4-16. Assume for this exercise that the detection phase of "development" includes defects discovered in work product reviews and in internal testing.

1. What does the data suggest about Project A's requirements management and product testing processes?
2. What additional information do you need to understand the significance of this data for your project?

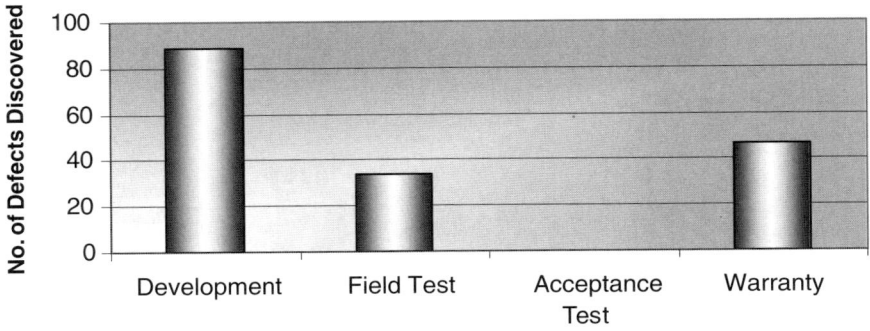

Figure 4-16 ● Project A's Detection Phase Data for Exercise 4-2a

Exercise 4-2b

Suppose the previous project's data looked instead like the data in Figure 4-17. Do you need any additional information to under-

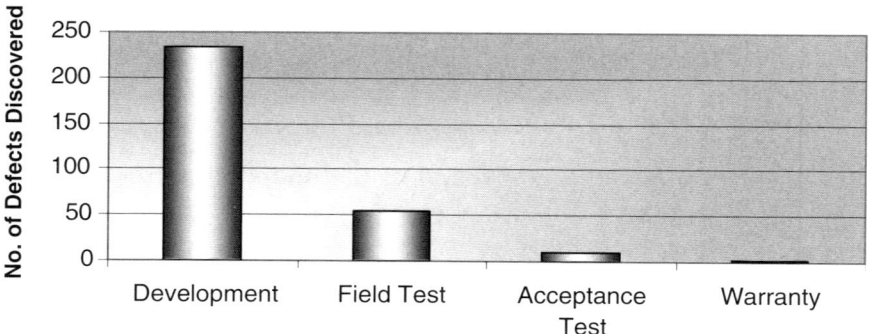

Figure 4-17 ■ Project A's Detection Phase Data for Exercise 4-2b

stand the significance of this data for your project? If so, what additional information do you need?

Exercise 4-3: Interpreting Injection Phase Data

Like detection phase data, injection phase data can tell you how well your development processes are working. This exercise asks you to probe the possible causes for, and extrapolate the implications of, injection phase data for a prior release.

Once again, you are the project manager for Version 2.0 of the OopsTryThis product. Looking at the archives for the Version 1.0 project, you come across the final injection phase report for the project closure meeting. Based on what you see in Figure 4-18, what can

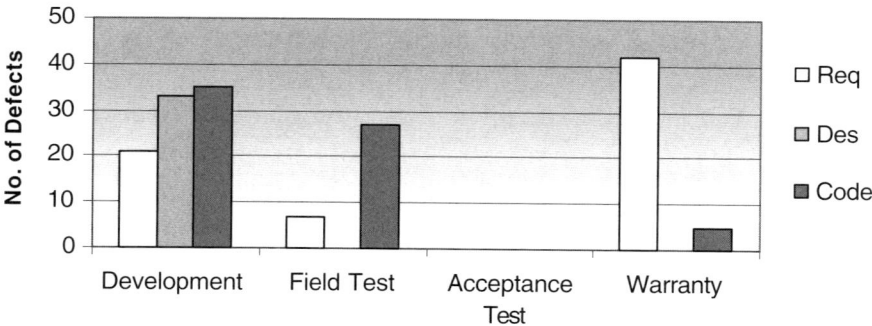

Figure 4-18 ■ Project A's Injection Phase Data for Exercise 4-3

you surmise about the requirements, design, and coding processes? What can you surmise about the testing processes?

Exercise 4-4: Applying Injection and Detection Phases

While injection and detection phases are typically used in initial product development cycles, they can just as easily be applied to commissioning, maintenance, or support. Suppose, for example, that when a product is released to a customer, that process involves four milestones:

- *Staging.* The product is installed in a test lab that simulates the customer environment.
- *Installation.* The product is installed and readied for use on the customer site.
- *Warranty.* For a period of 30 days the customer has unlimited, free access to all development and field service personnel to correct any problems with the product. User training is conducted on-site during this time.
- *Support.* After 30 days the customer can report problems and receive regularly scheduled updates.

Each of these can be called a phase. The entire development process preceding the staging phase can be considered one large phase, so let's call this initial phase "development."

Defects or problems that are not detected at the appropriate phase can be considered "injected" at that phase. So, for example:

- An error in the installation guide is not found in the staging phase but is discovered in the installation phase; this problem has an injection phase of staging and a detection phase of installation.
- The staging process found that a required hardware parameter setting was not documented in the installation manual; this problem has an injection phase of development (or documentation, if separate) and a detection phase of staging.

- Changes in the product were not reflected in the user guides shipped to the customer, resulting in several calls to the phone support specialists after the warranty period had expired; this problem was detected at the support phase and, strictly speaking, was injected by configuration management in development or documentation. The injection phase could also be assigned to the warranty phase, however, since the problem was not discovered during user training.

Review your own organization's injection and detection rates and then identify ways to mitigate the risks in your own projects, following these steps:

1. Review the customer-generated defect reports for a product in your organization.
2. From those reports, generate injection phase and detection phase categories.
3. Classify the reports and then generate a bar chart of the relative percentages of each category.
4. Suppose you were the project manager for the follow-on release of that product. What are the implications of the injection and detection phase data? What processes would you want to watch over more closely? What measures would you like to have and at what points would you take these measures?

Exercise 4-5: Reviewing Your Problem Report Tracking

1. Using the diagram in Figure 4-19, determine what categories of information you collect now and those that you would like to collect. A line item could be a category of information you require, a field name, or even a specific base measure.
2. Using Figure 4-20, identify the specific values for the tracking system. Again, these could be values you currently use or want to use. If the values are not self-explanatory, remember to provide an explanation of what they mean or when to use them.

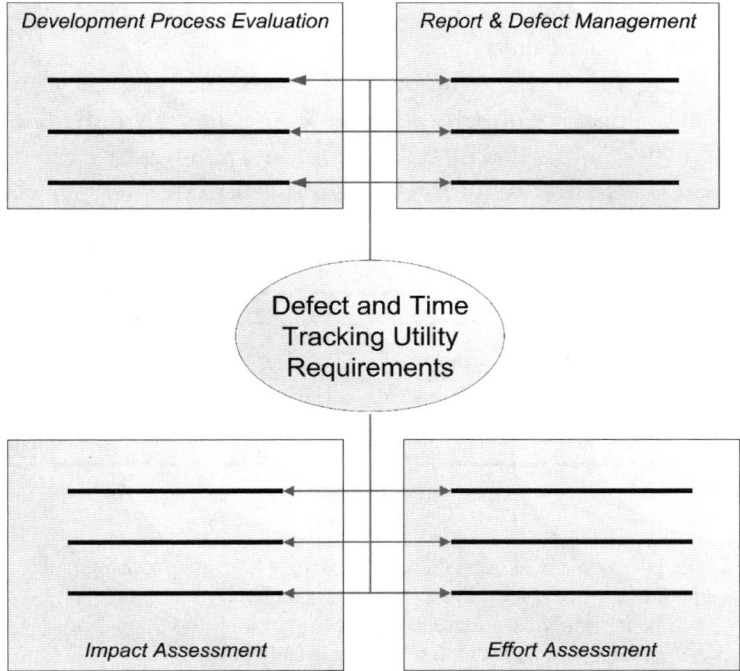

Figure 4-19 ● Template for Categories and Tracked Data

Category	Field	Values
Impact	Risk to Fix	High (Can only be tested on customer site), Medium (affected feature must be regression tested), Low (point test sufficient)

Figure 4-20 ● Sample Problem Tracking Field Description

Exercise 4-6: Personal Time Tracking

Before you tell your entire department to start logging their time in 15-minute increments, you ought to try it yourself. Accurate time logging isn't easy, and it's usually an eye-opener.

1. Think about the tasks you have to complete in a typical week, and code them into types (such as "WS" for prepare weekly status report or "TM" for team meetings).

2. Estimate how much time you will spend on each task over the next five days.
3. Using the form in Figure 4-21 (or something of your own choosing), spend five days recording all your time.
4. At the end of the fifth day, compute your actual direct time on tasks and the interruption and blocked times per task.

Personal Time Recording Log						
Task Keys	<key1>, <key2>					
Estimated Time for Tasks	<key1: time> <key2: time>, etc.					
Date	**Task**	**Start**	**Stop**	**Interrupt Time**	**Delta Time**	**Blocked Time**

The task keys are abbreviations for task types. Interruptions include phone calls, people walking into your office to chat, etc. The delta time is simply the difference between start and stop times, and includes both interruptions and blocks.

Figure 4-21 ■ Sample Personal Time Log

Exercise 4-7: A Project Team Exercise in Defect Injection and Risk Mitigation

For this exercise, you will need a team of people—your project team, a group of your peer software project managers, or maybe just a handful of developers and testers. The goal of the exercise is to identify causal relationships between events in your project workflow. So the first step in the exercise is to diagram the project's workflow on a whiteboard: the kinds of tasks, the flow of information and deliverables, and the milestones.

Once the workflow is laid out, start looking at the dependencies between tasks. If you and your team are familiar with process failure mode effect analysis (PFMEA) techniques, you could break into smaller groups and work out the process interdependencies and risks. If you and your team are not familiar with PFMEA, or if you want to keep this brainstorming session a bit more interactive, you can set up several matrices for looking at specific areas of the project.

1. Taking either phases or generic development tasks, generate a list of the kinds of problems that can occur in that phase or task.
2. Develop a list of causes for the problems and then determine if the effects of the causes will appear in that task or phase, in a subsequent task or phase, or both.
3. Identify the possible effects, and then categorize them into three or four main effect types.
4. Finally, determine the nature of the relationship between the cause and the effect. The sample matrix in Figure 4-22 uses two types of relationships: strong and moderate/low.
   a. Strong relationships mean that if the cause exists, the effect is likely to happen.
   b. Moderate or low relationships mean that the identified cause doesn't always produce the effect.

You can use typical group brainstorming tools such as affinity diagrams, interrelationship diagraphs, mind maps, and cause-effect diagrams. No matter how you develop the information, you should collect it all in one matrix. Figure 4-22 shows an Appearance – Cause – Effect matrix that combines all the information into one table. (To simplify the illustration, only a few aspects of the topic have been addressed in the matrix.)

Completing matrices for all your major development tasks or phases will give you a fairly comprehensive view of the project risks embedded in your workflow. From that set of matrices you can determine the project events and project processes that can contribute to product defects, schedule slips, and effort or cost overruns.

The next step is to get the team to prioritize these risks. Based on their experiences in projects to date and the kinds of issues they have experienced with the technical aspects of the workflow, you and your team can select those problems that they will likely encounter and identify risk mitigation strategies.

Effect will appear in:		Cause/Causal Event	Effect of Cause			
			Slippage	Injected defect	Misunderstanding that might inject a defect	Misunderstanding that might inject a process error
This task's phase		Requirement information not available	●	●	●	○
		Requirement information not correct	○	●	●	○
		New method in use (e.g., switch to use cases)	●	●	●	●
		Customer unavailable for review	●	●	○	○
		Insufficient time for customer review	○	●	○	○
		Customer requirements not traceable to software requirements	○	○	●	●
A later phase		Documentation incomplete	○	●	●	○
		Documentation ambiguous	○	●	●	○
		Requirements not reviewed for consistency with each other	○	●	●	○
		Missing requirements	○	●	●	○
● Strong causal relationship			○ Moderate or low causal relationship			

Figure 4-22 ● ACE Matrix (Appearance – Cause – Effect)

Since the information is already broken down by task type or phase, you can use the matrix to help define the details of injection and detection phase measures and measurement points. If you include time or effort in your effect analysis, you will be able to use the matrix to help define time logging categories or attributes (e.g., what kinds of events are legitimately logged under blocked time).

You can also combine risk or impact analysis with your causal analysis. Identify the types of impact you are interested in; in this example, it's lost time, lost productivity, etc. Figure 4-23 shows a Cause – Effect – Impact matrix that links causes to effects and links effects to the impact on the project. This information is useful in a number of ways. First, this type of matrix helps the entire team realize how dependent they are on each other's work. In Figure 4-23

Cause	Work Flow Effect	Project Impact			
		Lost Time	Rework	Schedule Delay	Lost Productivity
Error handling not specified in Use Case	Tester doesn't create test case for error handling	⊙	⊙	⊙	⊙
	Tester creates inappropriate test case	⊙	○	○	○
	Tester creates test cases that identify error handling issues that have to be resolved and retrofitted to product during product test	●	●	●	○
	Change Control Board can't determine if a defect report on error handling indicates a requirements failure	●	⊙	○	⊙
	Change Control Board can't determine importance of a defect report on error handling for ship criteria	●	⊙	○	⊙
	Designer does not include error handling in design	⊙	⊙	⊙	⊙
	Designer includes error handling that doesn't meet customer expectations	●	●	●	○
	Developer invents error handling algorithms during coding	●	●	●	○
	Invented error handling assumes interfaces not specified/not developed in other components	○	○	○	○
	Documentation team not aware of user interface changes for error handling until final correlation of guides with product	○	●	⊙	⊙

● **Strong possibility**   ○ **Moderate possibility**   ⊙ **Low possibility**

Figure 4-23 ● CEI Matrix (Cause – Effect – Impact)

you can see how an omission in a use case developed in the requirements stage can cause different problems for the rest of the development team.

Second, the matrix can be used proactively as a risk management tool. If you see one of the effects, you know to look for its possible impacts. You will also know to scrutinize your time and defect measures for any signs of possible impact. Finally, some of the entries in the matrix will identify the process deficiencies that underlie defects and schedule slips. In effect, the matrix functions as a root cause checklist that identifies problems in your project's processes before they become crises.

Measuring Up:
Historical Data and Indicators

The good news is that your previous three software development projects were successful. The bad news is that the VP of Engineering expects the trend to continue. There's no guarantee that your next software development project will be a success, even if you work in a high-maturity level organization. You do, however, have an advantage in your fourth project that you did not have in the first one: you have historical data to work with.

Having historical data at your disposal can help you in a number of ways. It can show you where your challenges lie compared to previous projects. It can show how well you addressed those challenges. And, of course, that data can be used to show how much project efficiency and product quality have improved under your stewardship . . . .

In previous chapters you learned how to apply and interpret run rate data for defects and time or effort, and you learned how to analyze project performance data. Those chapters focused on putting the information to immediate use: diagnosing a quality problem, identifying risks to the schedule, etc. The measurements presented in this chapter can be applied in the same way, but they can also be used retrospectively in comparative measures of trends and improvements across projects.

● USING PREVIOUS RELEASE DATA

Defect incidence per release is a derived measure that in turn provides the data for a comparative indicator. The number of defects in a release, either in total or as differentiated by project phase or milestone, is compared across several releases in an attempt to identify any trends in defect incidence. Figure 5-1 presents an example of such a comparison of historical release data.

The similarity of the trends in run rates for the three projects is readily apparent. Based on what you have learned in previous chapters, you have probably already started asking the pertinent questions:

➡ Is there sufficient similarity in the products?
- Are these projects developing separate software products?
- Are they different development efforts for the same product? (For example, are Projects 2 and 3 enhancement efforts for the product developed in Project 1?)

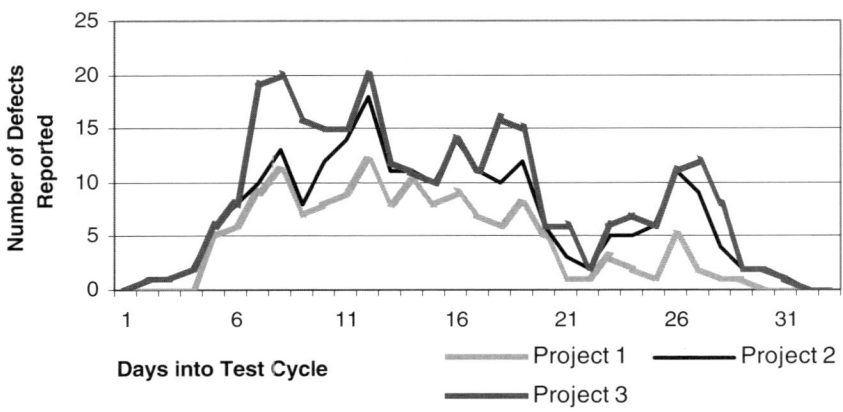

Figure 5-1 ● Historical Test Cycle Data for Three Projects

➡ Is there sufficient similarity in the processes?
  • Were the same development and test processes used for the three projects?
  • Were the project schedules similar, at least with respect to the amount of time allocated for testing?
  • Were these projects staffed similarly in terms of number of resources and skill levels?
➡ Would an attribute analysis show significant disparities?
  • Do the defects recorded for all three projects show similar patterns in the injection phase? If not, would the injection phase data shed any light on the different rates for Projects 2 and 3?
  • What would the problem report status analysis show?
  • What would an analysis of defects by component show?

The point, of course, is that it's very easy to graphically compare data from different projects without actually providing any insight into the data. Be cautious about making comparisons across a small number of projects, and make sure that most of the following conditions are met:

  • The products are the same type. (Don't mix embedded software projects with web application projects.)
  • Development and test processes are the same or similar.
  • Project schedules are comparable given the scope of the effort.

If these conditions are met, then comparisons are both legitimate and useful. Assuming you have enough releases to work with, you can generate historical averages and determine if the current project is at least performing within historical norms. Figure 5-2 was created using a year's worth of release data and four release cycles. The average defect rate per day and the average deviation were calculated across all previous releases, giving the historical high/low deviations and the historical average. The current defect rates were plotted against these values for the sample period of 17 days.

Because development cycles are affected by so many variables, it is not really legitimate to consider this statistical process control.

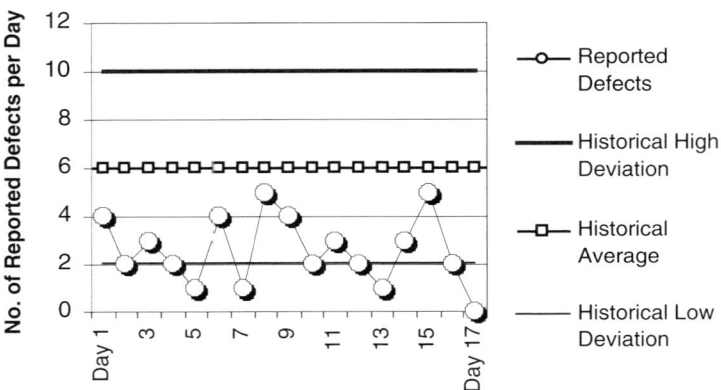

Figure 5-2 ■ Comparing Current and Historical Run Rates

For statistical process control, you would need more than three projects and you would need to know that all the relevant processes were consistently and universally applied in the projects. Comparing defect rates across multiple releases is nonetheless a legitimate trend indicator, provided that you do not draw hasty conclusions from the data.

The rate of reported defects for the current release in Figure 5-2 looks like good news: the current release looks very clean. Bear in mind, however, that the same trend could be generated from a truncated test schedule that prevented full coverage, a set of requirements that was so ambiguous that requirement validation was a matter of guesswork rather than validation, or just plain shoddy testing and defect reporting. There's no reason why you can't draw conclusions from limited data, but you must know what could cause the data to appear the way it does and you must do your research to determine which of those possibilities affect the data.

■ USING INDICATORS

Derived measures involve some level of uncertainty. If certain factors can cause variation from one measurement to the next, even small differences can affect the value of the derived measure. This is why it is so important to interrogate the data for the "why" and not just look at the "what." When you look into the environmental factors behind the data (such as blocked time or defect-ridden components), you uncover the reasons for variations and can address those reasons as necessary.

Indicators attempt to flatten the effect of local variations between projects by combining derived measurement data over extended periods of time, such as multiple projects or different releases. Taking a series of derived measures over time balances the localized effect of variance with a larger and perhaps more diverse sample set. Strictly speaking, indicators are intended to identify deviations from expected norms. Indicators such as phase containment or cost of poor quality are statistically significant and useful only if the sample set is quite large and the project execution environment is the same across all the projects.

Nonetheless, indicators can be used heuristically even when the sample set is small. Remember that heuristic measures give us a qualitative assessment of the product or process. As long as you recognize the limits to what you can surmise from limited data, you can use the indicators to help you evaluate your productivity and product quality across projects.

● PHASE CONTAINMENT INDICATOR

Phase containment is the percentage of defects discovered per "phase" in a software development lifecycle. The rationale behind the indicator is that the cost to find and fix a defect increases the further along the lifecycle you go. The purpose of this indicator is to determine whether defects are being discovered at the optimum moment in the lifecycle.

Identifying detection phases for this indicator is relatively simple—they should match your project or development lifecycle phases. Injection phases may be more difficult to define. For example, iterative development lacks the clear distinctions between requirements, design, code, and test that are found in the waterfall models. If you can't easily track injection to a specific iteration, then it's perfectly acceptable to define phases as activity types, such as initial customer requirement specification, functional description, coding, etc.

In its simplest form, phase containment is simply the number of defects detected at a given measurement point expressed as a percentage of the total known defects. There's a catch here, of course: as you work through the project, you will probably discover more defects. That means a phase containment value obtained for peer reviews before test will differ from the phase containment value for peer reviews obtained after the test cycle. Similarly, the phase containment value for the test effort will probably change after the release date as defect reports come in from the customer sites.

As a result, consistency should be your primary concern when using this indicator. Collect your defect data in the same phases and at the same measurement points across the various projects. If the last phase of Project A is an arbitrary six months after first customer ship and the last phase of Project B is end-of-warranty for the last customer still using the product, you can legitimately compare their phase containments for the end of the test cycle. You cannot legitimately compare the phase containment for the entire project lifecycle because the unit of measure—the lifecycle—differs between the two projects.

Sample Application

Ideally, phase containment data is always supplemented with injection phase data. This provides some additional diagnostic information about the containment values. For example, the number of detected defects, per phase, can be divided into their injection phases using a stacked percentage bar chart. Alternatively, if you want to emphasize one aspect of injection or detection, you can use an area column chart.

Figure 5-3 shows where defects were injected and detected in a release cycle. The phases are two iterations: a beta test and a customer acceptance test. The defect injection points are the requirements, design, and coding processes. The injection point "requirements" is singled out using columns rather than area to emphasize

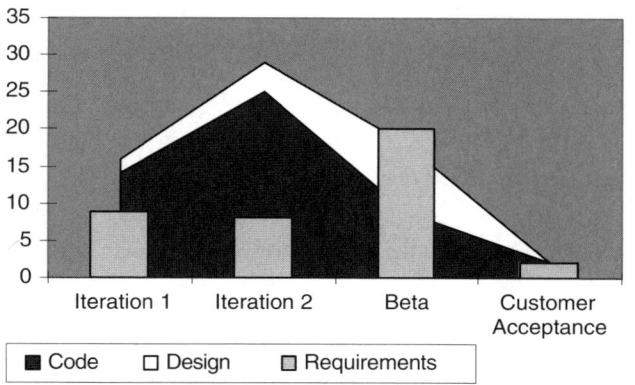

Figure 5-3 ● Combining Injection Phase and Detection Phase

whether the iterations were effective at removing requirements defects. The high number of requirements defects in the beta test suggests that they were not, pointing out an opportunity to improve the iterative processes in the future. Defects due to design errors also are higher in the beta test than in the iterations. This suggests that iteration phase planning in the future needs to stress more significant use of the product by the customer during the iteration period.

● DEFECT DENSITY INDICATOR

Strictly speaking, defect density is an incidence measure. Typically, it represents the number of defects per some size unit: lines of code, function points, objects, etc. Properly implemented, a size measure should distinguish between states of the source code.

Whether you use function points, lines of code, or some other unit, it is helpful to know how many of the lines or function points are new, how many were modified, how many have been deleted, and how many were reused or unmodified. Each of these represents a different risk to defect injection. New lines and modified lines can introduce completely new defects. Modified and removed lines can break existing functionality and cause defects in areas that have already been validated. Removed lines can remove functionality, and thus result in regression.

However, it is often difficult even with advanced source control packages to get this level of detailed information. Since most commercial source code management utility packages can compute the total lines of code for you relatively easily, we'll use lines of code as our size unit. Defect density will be calculated as the number of defects per 1,000 lines of executable source code (LOC).

Your LOC measures should initially include total lines (total LOC) and the difference between the current product and some previous baseline (delta LOC). If your source code management tool can provide you the total lines of code by component (or "project"), you may want to take advantage of this added level of detail in any component analyses you do.

Measurement points for defect density typically include the following:

- Defect density by project phase
- Defect density by build
- Defect density by release
- Defect density by component.

If these measurement points look familiar, they should. They are the typical measurement points for derived defect measures or phase containment. In fact, defect density is sometimes used as the unit of measure in phase containment. In this approach, the phase containment value is based on the defect density at that measurement point. The total number of known defects at a given phase and measurement point is divided by the size to obtain the defect density. When the next measurement point arrives, a new defect density is calculated based on the new total number of defects and total size.

The comparison of the densities between measurement points gives you comparative phase containment. A high defect density after peer reviews and a lower defect density after test are good news.

Many organizations also use defect density as an indicator of product quality or process efficiency. With a sufficiently large set of project data to draw from, and with a moderately consistent development process, such applications are valid. If those two conditions aren't met, as they generally are not in low-maturity organizations, be wary of trying to make defect density a quality or efficiency indicator.

First, defect density is a politically charged measurement. Defect density *per se* does not distinguish between causes for the defects. Development teams will often object to its use as a quality or efficiency indicator because management often assigns the blame to the development team. For example, the indicator does not distinguish between coding mistakes by developers, defects caused by compressed development schedules and overtime, and defects caused by poor requirements from the customer.

Second, a reasonable argument can be made that density is only half the picture. The complexity of the code or the technological complexity of the system as a whole can have a significant impact on the number of defects injected into the product. These same factors, as well as the project schedule, can increase the number of defects and thus increase the defect density.

Sample Application

The complex chart in Figure 5-4 illustrates the two different uses of defect density. The defect density for all lines in the product was computed for three releases. Shown as the top area, this rate has been declining across the releases. Each release increased the number of lines of code, and, of course, defects were discovered in each release. The larger area shows the defect density for just the new lines of code for each release. It is significantly higher than for the total product, but that is also to be expected. The good news in this chart is that the defect density for each release is declining with each release.

The columns in Figure 5-4 track the defect density as a function of time. The left-hand column shows the defect density that was computed at the end of the test cycle. The right-hand column shows the value of defect density after three months in the field. The post-

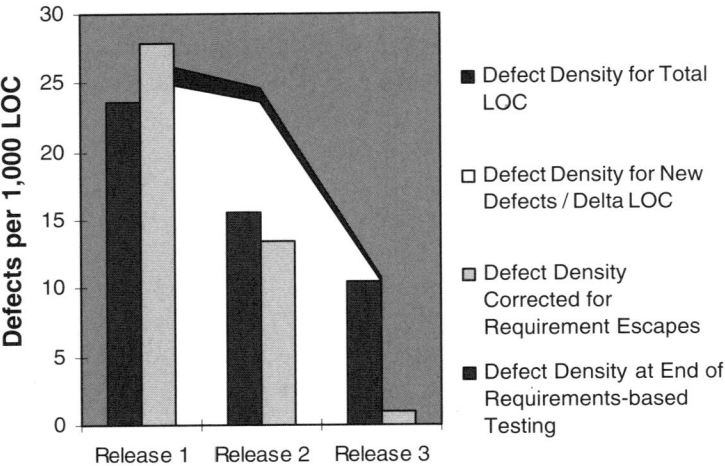

The areas show the defect density for the total lines of code in the product (total LOC), as well as for the difference in lines of code between releases (delta LOC). The columns indicate the defect density that was calculated at the end of testing, and the defect density calculated for the product after three months in the field (corrected for requirement escapes).

Figure 5-4 ● Defect Density for Three Releases

test defect density has improved across the three releases, which suggests that the overall containment has improved across the three releases as well.

● A TWIST ON THE EARNED VALUE INDICATOR

There are two possible applications of earned value. You are probably already familiar with one: using earned value as a project-level productivity or plan compliance indicator. Since earned value is computed based on allocated time per task, it functions both as a cost measure (time) and as a progress measure (tasks completed). From the project perspective, the "value" earned in the project is the successful completion of the planned tasks at the planned cost. But is this the only value your project team provides?

There are probably very few minutes in a day when your development or test teams aren't providing some valuable service to *some* sector of the organization. You know in your heart that your team members are being good corporate citizens when they help out another department, even if you complain to your manager that your project's time and resources are being squandered on another project that isn't even paying for the assistance.

Unless you work in a very sequestered environment, you will lose some percentage of your resources, officially or unofficially, to tasks that are taken for granted as part of the software engineering workday but aren't in your work breakdown structure. This is where the second application of earned value is helpful: it gives you an accurate picture of resource utilization by expanding the definition of value to include unavoidable contributions to other parts of the organization.

These unplanned activities are where your biggest risk lies with respect to schedule and productivity, and thus with earned value. Accordingly, it is important to recognize and focus on "team-level earned value." Team-level earned value combines the time categorizations introduced in Chapters 3 and 4 with the basic concepts of project-level earned value: tasks, time, and percent complete. This approach to "value" will help you:

- Determine where your project teams are actually spending their time
- Determine what categories of non-project effort are unavoidable in your environment
- Factor this unavoidable effort into your estimates
- Manage risks to your project-level earned value.

Sample Application

Based on the number of hours planned into a project and the estimated hours per task, it is possible to compute the percent complete that each task represents. This percent complete can then be tracked by any appropriate time period to generate a graphical display of the project's earned value for that segment of the project.

For example, suppose on your plan the systems engineering team has been assigned a series of requirements-related tasks spanning five weeks. Based on the completion rate of the tasks, your project-level earned value tracks lower than you had planned (see Figure 5-5).

Looking at the cumulative hours spent on the project by the systems engineers (see Figure 5-6), you can see that it is taking longer than expected to complete tasks. The question is, why is it taking longer than expected? Even though your project's resource allocation model probably includes time off for vacation, sick time, and general administrative overhead, it probably does not include a percentage for the actual day-to-day interruptions and obstacles that any development organization encounters. You need to determine this percentage as best you can. Some of this time is no doubt lost to activities that don't serve your project plan but cannot be avoided. That time needs to be accounted for somehow.

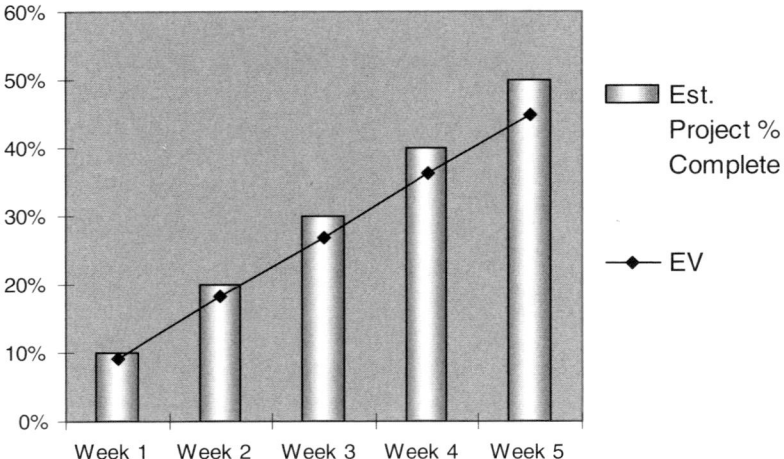

Figure 5-5 ■ Project-level Earned Value for the Systems Engineering Segment

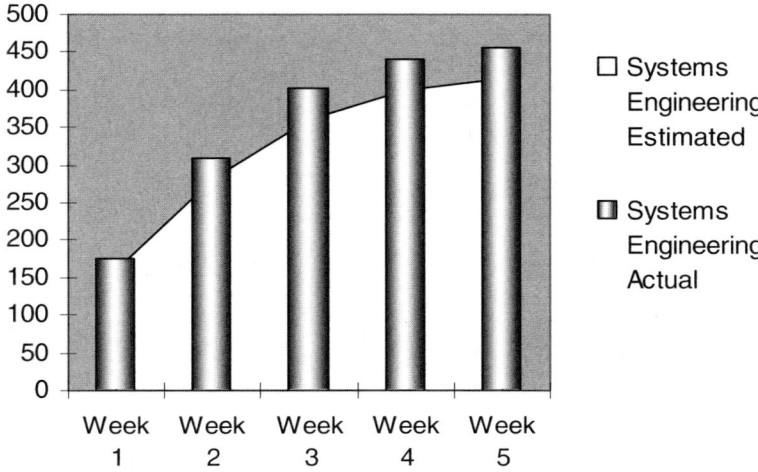

Figure 5-6 ● Cumulative Hours Charged in Systems Engineering Segment

This is where time categorization is useful. For example, Figure 5-7 shows some typical categories of tasks in a software development organization. Not all of these may be project-related—for example, answering support calls or performing maintenance on a previous release. Nonetheless, these are still important tasks, and would be measured under the category of "service time." Project-related task time, including any blocked time, would be measured under "planned time." Blocked time includes all blockages for planned or service tasks. Lost time is what is left in the workweek.

It's important to remember that service, blocked, and lost time may not always be predictable but may always be present in your project. When your project time is measured in the hundreds of hours, a few lost or blocked hours won't have much of an effect. When your planned hours start to decrease, however, service and blocked time can have a more serious effect on your plans.

To illustrate using the systems engineering example, Figure 5–8 shows that the planned hours for the systems engineering team de-

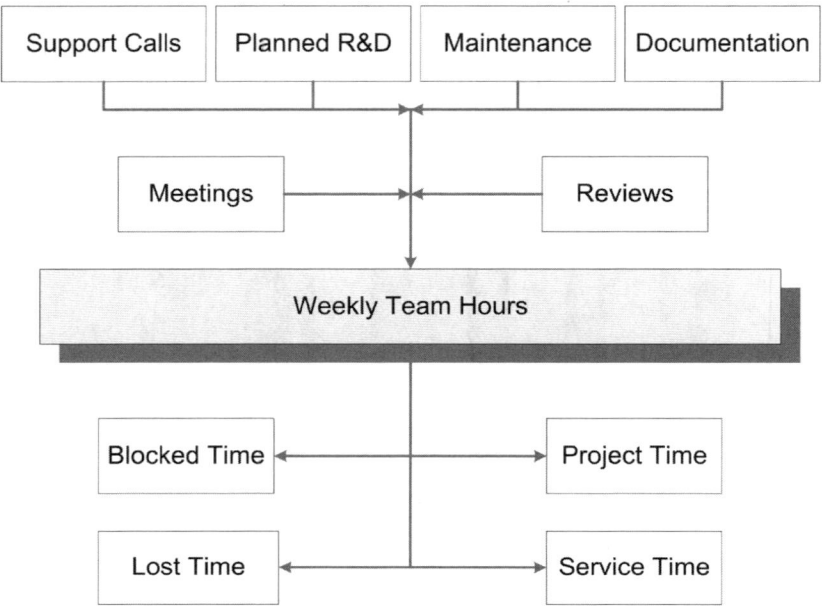

Figure 5-7 ■ Factors Affecting Team Productivity and Time Tracking
        Categories

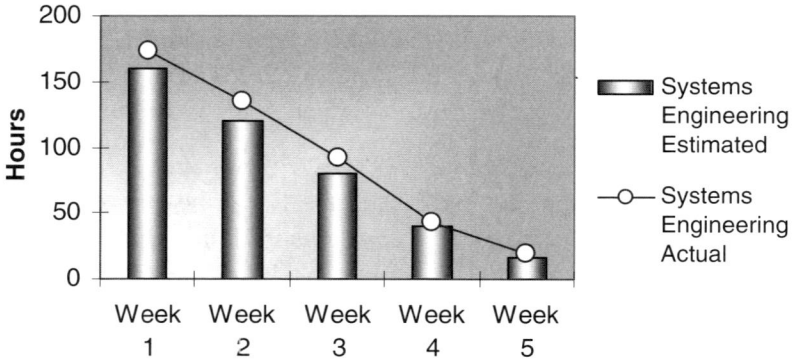

Figure 5-8 ■ Estimated and Actual Hourly Rates for Systems Engineering
        Segment

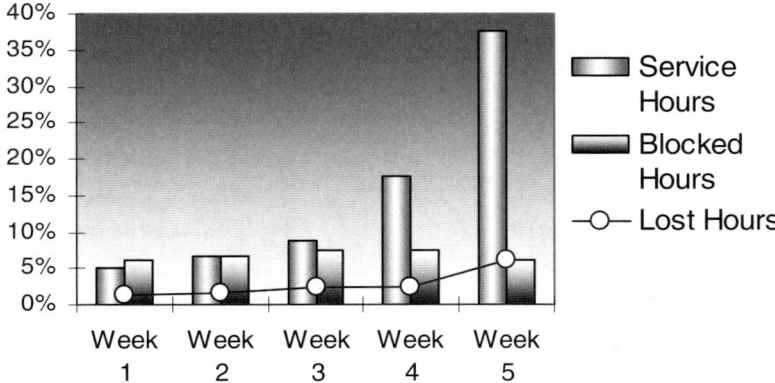

Figure 5-9 ● Non-project Time in Systems Engineering Segment

creased from one week to the next. In the same period, the relative percentage of service and lost time increased (see Figure 5-9). What is a minor interruption in Week 1 becomes a major interruption in Week 5, simply because there are fewer planned hours (and/or resources) to absorb the unplanned time without affecting the project.

It's important to note that the service time is probably not something you will be able to change; you can only adapt to it. If, on average, the system engineering team spends five percent of its time doing service tasks such as support or maintenance, then that needs to be factored into your resource allocation planning and thus into your earned value calculations.

This becomes especially important when different groups have tasks that are planned in parallel. Figure 5-10 shows how the software engineering effort was adversely affected by the drops in the systems engineering earned value. Even though the systems engineering team tracked close to expectations in Week 5, the effect of previous problems had already pushed the software engineering effort some 30 hours over plan. If your planned earned value hasn't taken into account the unavoidable service time for the software engineers, you can expect that gap to widen in the weeks ahead. Of

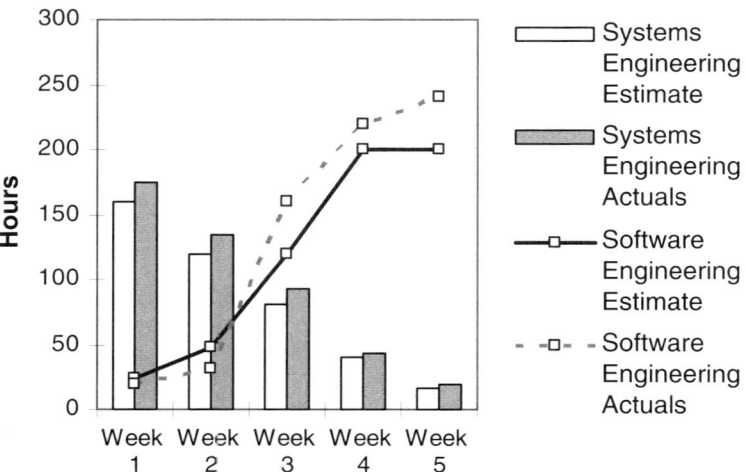

Figure 5-10 ▪ Effort for Systems and Software Engineering Segments

course, missing your earned value targets also increases your cost differentials, as the comparison of Budgeted Cost of Work Performed with Actual Cost of Work Performed in Figure 5-11 shows.

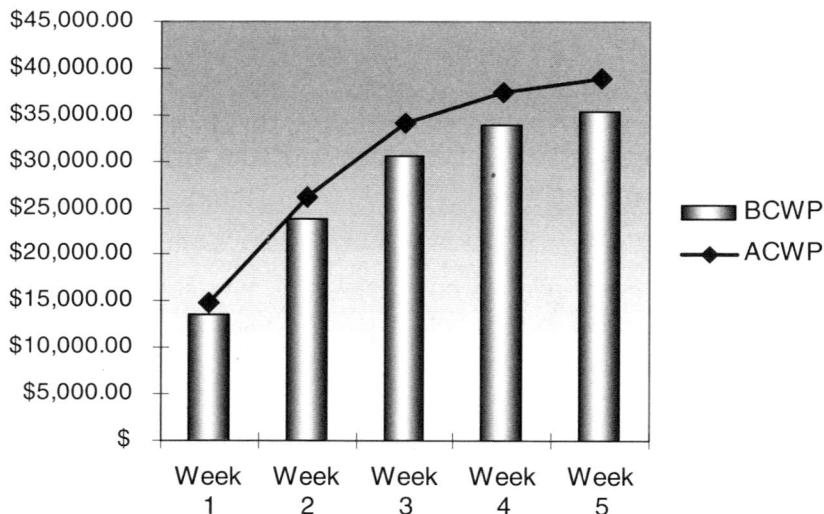

Figure 5-11 ▪ Budgeted vs. Actual Cost of Work Performed for Systems Engineering Segment

● COST OF QUALITY/POOR QUALITY INDICATOR

Cost of quality can be looked at in two different ways: as the cost of ensuring quality, and as the costs associated with a poor-quality product. The two perspectives are not always separated in the literature about cost of quality. Cost-of-quality measures usually emphasize the cost of quality control or quality assurance. Cost-of-poor-quality measures usually emphasize the time and productivity lost when you test out defects rather than remove them using formal design methods and reviews.

Cost of quality or cost of poor quality is generally one of the last indicators implemented in corporate-sponsored software metrics programs. Properly implemented, the indicator combines financial data for the entire product lifecycle with defect and resource time/cost data for some sections of the product lifecycle. It therefore requires the kind of coordination between departments that generally only high-maturity level organizations can achieve.

Nevertheless, the cost of quality and the cost of poor quality are useful indicators even if the financial data is limited and the time/cost data is an estimate based on project plan durations and resource transfer rates. In effect, cost of quality looks at how much we spent to do as good a job as we did with the product, while cost of poor quality shows what we might have saved if we'd done a better job in the first place. Included in cost of quality are the costs for appraisal and preventive tasks: peer reviews, formal design tasks, in-house testing, and possibly even customer beta testing. Included in the cost of poor quality are the cost of defect detection and repair, generally focusing on the costs in the testing and post-shipment phases.

Cost Types and Categories

Before you can legitimately calculate cost of quality or the cost of poor quality, you need to determine the appropriate cost categories and rates. Costs can be calculated in many ways, and you would do well to learn how your organization (especially the finance group) calculates cost. While the names for these categories may differ from one organization to another, these are the typical rates:

- Loaded rate
- Transfer rate
- Project rate
- Charged rate.

The loaded rate is the cost to the company of an employee. It includes actual costs like salary and benefits and may be an hourly or yearly value. In addition, it includes prorated costs or "taxes" for facilities, non-productive time and resources, capital, benefits, etc.

The transfer rate is the hourly rate one department charges to provide resources to another department. It's often the rate used to determine project cost overruns, although the actual costs may be much higher depending on the nature of the problem.

Some projects will have project-specific charge rates. When the project is partly or wholly funded by the customer, there's the opportunity to charge the customer higher rates for certain types of skills. In a case like this, you might find that your database architect has a price tag of $140 per hour, while your testers are charged at the normal transfer rate. Obviously, you'll need to know the per-resource values when calculating costs for tasks in a project as well as the costs of delays or slippages.

Finally, if you are using contractors or consultants, you need to take into account charge rates. Contractors and consultants have a higher per-hour salary rate, but they do not consume company benefits. Finance may cost them out as if they were full-fledged loaded-cost employees, it may prorate their loaded costs to remove benefits but tack on facility costs, or it may simply cost them out by hourly wage. Be sure to find out which of these options is used, since it will affect the accuracy of any calculations you make for costs where contractors or consultants are involved.

You will also need to categorize costs by the kind of activity involved. Choose your categories based on what you want to accomplish with your cost measures and how easily you can get the data. If you categorize costs by phase, you will know roughly what it costs to complete the major phases of a project. Phases could be iterations, major builds, or the traditional "waterfall four" of requirements, design, code, and test. Pick categories that match your methods, lifecycle, and project planning milestones. This will give you a high-level understanding of the project costs per phase using one or more of the cost calculations.

Another approach to cost measurement uses labor types. Divide costs into the typical categories of direct labor, appraisal labor, preventive labor, and overhead:

- Direct labor is any time spent on formal deliverables for the release or project, such as writing specifications, participating in design discussions or meetings, coding, testing, etc.
- Appraisal labor is any time spent analyzing the ability of the product to meet requirements. Appraisal labor is aimed at assessing how good the product or process is. This would include any formal reviews, usability testing, customer acceptance testing, etc.
- Preventive labor is directed toward preventing defects or process failures in the first place. In an immature development organization, it is unlikely that you will be racking up any significant preventive costs, since you are probably not doing formal or mathematical design validation or failure mode and effects analysis.
- Overhead can be a catch-all for everything else. It always includes time spent on emails, company-wide meetings, moving offices, etc. You may choose to distinguish blocked time from overhead time in your labor categories.

Figures 5-12 and 5-13 show how task time can be converted to cost categories. The timesheet identifies tasks, which must be

Time Sheet for Joe James			Wk. Ending 8/5/10		
	Mon	Tue	Wed	Thu	Fri
Writing design doc for Feature B	7		3		
Development Feature A		5			6
Fix for Problem 3452	1		1		
Fix for problem 4571				8	2
Requirements review for release ZZZ		1			
Staff Meeting			1.5		

Figure 5-12 ● Sample Employee Timesheet

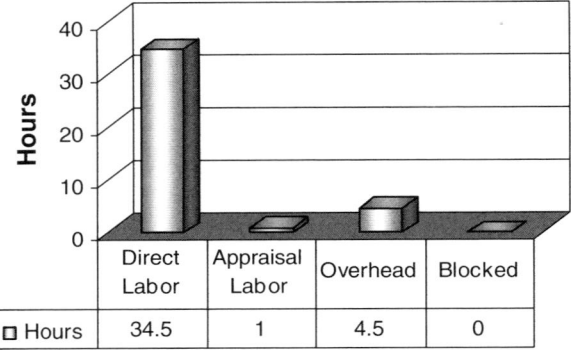

	Direct Labor	Appraisal Labor	Overhead	Blocked
☐ Hours	34.5	1	4.5	0

Figure 5-13 ■ Applying Cost Categories to Time Data

converted into cost types. Only the requirements review on the timesheet counts as an appraisal cost. The rest is either direct labor or overhead.

When more than one resource is involved in a task, you determine the costs by combining under the appropriate categories the hours each resource charged to the task. For example, in Figure 5-14, the transfer rate is $80 per hour. The total task transfer cost is the

Task	Actual	Blocks	Resources	Total Task Transfer Cost	Per Resource Transfer Cost	Total Task Hidden Cost
Test Prep	8	0	4	$ 640	$ 160	$ -
Regression						
Component 1	6	3	1	$ 480	$ 480	$ 240
Component 2	6		1	$ 480	$ 480	$ -
TC Development						
Feature A	24	10	1	$ 1,920	$ 1,920	$ 800
Feature B	12		1	$ 960	$ 960	$ -
Feature C	20		2	$ 1,600	$ 800	$ -
Initial Testing						
Feature A	32	40	2	$ 2,560	$ 1,280	$ 6,400
Feature B	16	4	1	$ 1,280	$ 1,280	$ 320
Feature C	24		1	$ 1,920	$ 1,920	$ -

Figure 5-14 ■ Transfer and Hidden Costs for Some Testing Tasks actual hours multiplied by the transfer rate. The per-resource transfer cost factors in the number of resources. Since the blocked hours represent time when all resources were blocked, total-task hidden cost is computed as the number of blocked hours (blocks) multiplied by the number of resources, multiplied in turn by the transfer rate.

Sample Application: Cost of Poor Quality

The cost of poor quality is generally easier to implement because it requires time and cost data only for defect discovery and repair. Figure 5-15 is based on average task times and the actual number of defects to date in the release. Using the timesheet data, the project manager has been able to compute the average cost for a developer to fix a defect (average time to fix costs). The project manager has also been able to compute the average cycle time, that is, the average total hours the project team spends to find a problem, fix it, build the software, and retest the software (average total cycle time costs).

A defect costs, on average, about $1,120 of developer time and $2,960 of the team's time. To date, the expense on defects has been $19,832, or roughly the equivalent of six person-weeks that could have been spent on more "productive" tasks.

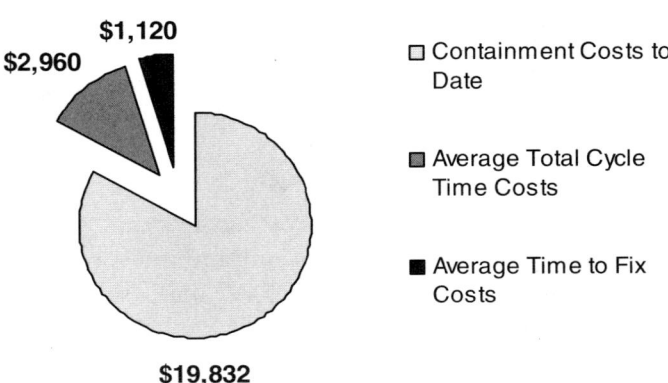

Figure 5-15 ● Cost of Poor Quality Example

Sample Application: Combining Cost of Poor Quality with Earned Value

For this example, we'll use the following task categories and base measures:

- *Research*—time spent reviewing documents, in formal reviews, and discussions
- *Development*—time spent in FMEA, test case development, automation development; time spent preparing for drops
- *Execution*—time spent executing tests, logging defects
- *Blockage*—time lost from main task because of delayed deliverables, waiting on builds or fixes
- *Rework*—time lost from main task because of bad fixes that have to be retested, or test cases that have to be rewritten
- *eTT*—estimated time for a given task
- *aTT*—actual time for a given task
- *TFC*—transfer cost ($85.00 per hour)
- *TP*—time period (one week, whole release, one category of task, etc.)
- *Tb*—actual time spent blocked
- *Tr*—actual time spent in rework.

We'll calculate the earned-value variance first without considering the cost of poor quality. The calculations are:

- **eEV**
  –Estimated earned value
  –(SUM eTT for all tasks in TP) * $85
- **aEV**
  –Actual earned value
  –(SUM aTT for all tasks in TP) * $85

Using the data in Figure 5-16, we can illustrate the estimation accuracy (shown in Figure 5-17) and compute the earned-value variance (shown in Figure 5-18). The estimated and actual earned values are computed this way:

eEV = (SUM B4:B6 + SUM D4:D6 + SUM F4:F6) * $85 = $10,200.00

1	A	B	C	D	E	F	G
2		Week 1		Week 2		Week 3	
3		Est.	Act.	Est.	Act.	Est.	Act.
4	Research	30	20	5	5	0	0
5	Development	10	10	20	10	5	5
6	Execution	0	0	15	10	35	10
7	Blockage	0	10	0	15	0	10
8	Rework	0	0	0	0	0	15

Figure 5-16 ● Data for Estimated and Actual Earned Value

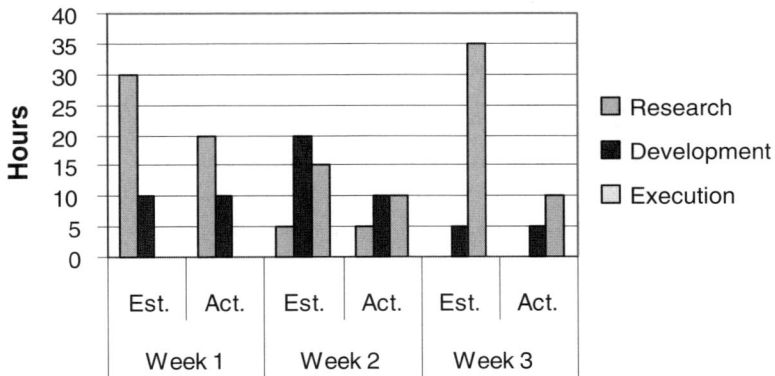

Figure 5-17 ● Estimation Accuracy for Task Categories

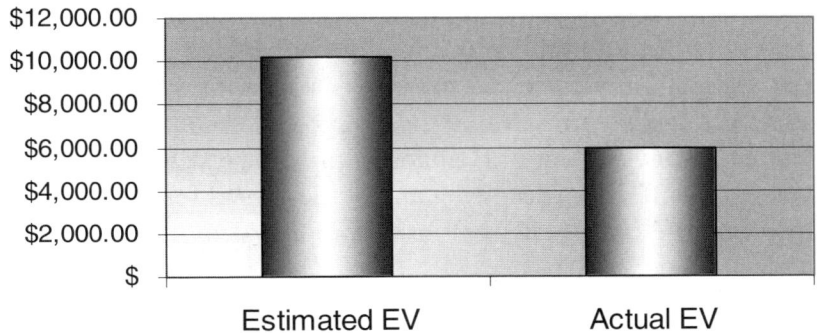

Figure 5-18 ● Earned Value Variance (COpQ not included) for
Weeks 1–3

aEV = (SUM C4:C6 + SUM E4:E6 + SUM G4:G6) * $85 =
$5,950.00

If we want to factor in the cost of poor quality, we have to use slightly different variables and calculations. The data is the same as used above:

- **eEV**
  - Estimated earned value
  - (SUM eTT for all tasks in TP) * $85
- **aEE**
  - Actual effort expended
  - ((SUM aTT for all tasks in TP) + (SUM Tb and Tr)) * $85
- **COpQ**
  - Cost of poor quality
  - (SUM Tb and Tr for all tasks in TP) * $85
- **aEVCOpQ**
  - Actual earned value with poor quality costs
  - aEE – COpQ

eEV = (SUM B4:B6 + SUM D4:D6 + SUM F4:F6) * $85 =
$10,200.00

aEE = (SUM C4:C8 + SUM E4:E8 + SUM G4:G8) * $85 =
$10,200.00

COpQ = (SUM C7:C8 + SUM E7:E8 + SUM G7:G8) * $85 =
$4,250.00

aEVCOpQ = (aEE – COpQ) = $5,950.00

When the results of the calculations are graphically displayed, it is clear how blocked time and rework time have adversely affected the project. Figure 5-19 shows that the cost of poor quality is almost equal to the actual earned value for the project. Charts like this show the return on investment of changes to project processes or interdepartmental interfaces. Addressing any of the causes for blocked time, or lowering the defect rate, will have a direct, demonstrable impact on earned value.

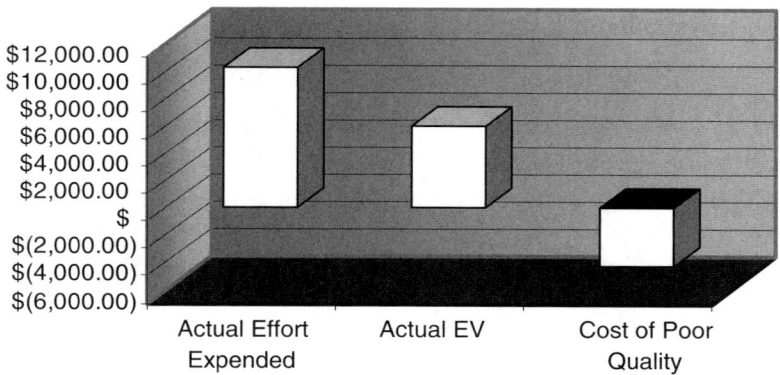

Figure 5-19 ● Earned Value Corrected for Cost of Poor Quality

● PUTTING THE PIECES TOGETHER

Cost charts like those in Figures 5-15 and 5-19 often raise more questions than they answer. Is the cost to date reasonable or unreasonable? Is there anything special about the kinds of defects discovered to date that has contributed to this cost? Is it fair to use an average of costs for defects—that is, is the defect-type profile for this release the same as in previous releases? Since there will always be some defects found in testing, how much of that containment cost to date is really lost productivity that could have been applied elsewhere?

These are all good questions, and if you have implemented all the measures discussed so far, you're actually in a position to answer them. The questions are all focused on the legitimacy of the cost indicator and the legitimacy of this particular measurement. They can be paraphrased into three slightly more abstract questions:

→ Is the cost data reasonable within historical norms?
→ Is this release similar enough to other releases that we can draw conclusions from comparisons with other releases?
→ Is the defect cost impacting other tasks?

To answer the first question, you should have historical cost data, as one would expect in the case of an indicator. But let's suppose for the sake of illustration that this is the first time you've computed cost of poor quality. This constraint means that you can't answer that first question "on its own terms" and at the appropriate level of abstraction. You can answer it indirectly, however. If you can show that the current release is like previous releases at the indicator and derived-measure levels, you have indirectly answered the first question. Of course, this is also the way to answer the second question.

To answer the second question, you can use defect run rates for previous releases, defect density per delta lines of code, and injection phase data. So let's assume for the sake of illustration that you are trying to answer these questions for a current release, and that you have data from two previous releases, Release A and Release B.

Figure 5-20 shows that the current release defect rate data is close to the rates for the two previous releases. Figure 5-21 indicates that the current release is also similar to those two releases in its defect density for the new lines of code in the release. Finally, Figure 5-22 suggests that the current release is tracking close to Release B with respect to injection phase. The average times for defect management computed from Releases A and B, therefore, can reasonably be applied to the current release.

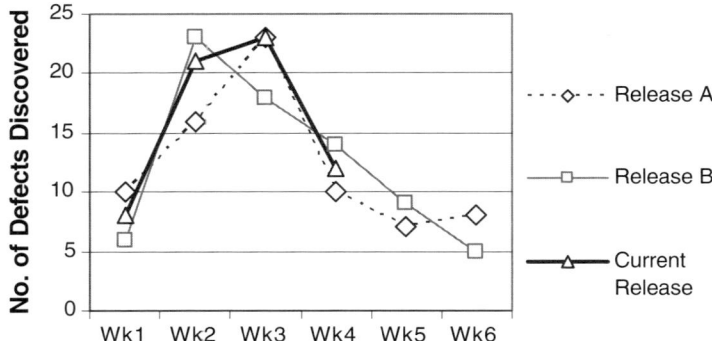

Figure 5-20 ■ Comparing Defect Run Rates across Three Releases

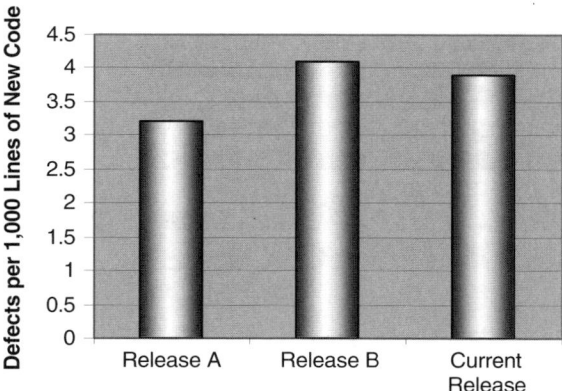

Figure 5-21 ● Defect Density for Three Releases

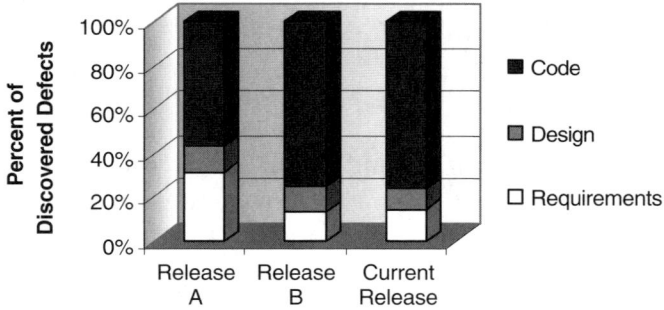

Figure 5-22 ● Defect Profile across Releases

What about the third question? How can we determine if there is any real impact on other project tasks? First, let's consider an indirect approach to the answer. The current release is similar to the previous releases in defect rate, defect density, and defect injection phase. If the current release was planned and resourced in ways similar to the previous two releases, then the current defect rate could have the same effect on the release schedule as it did in previous releases. If

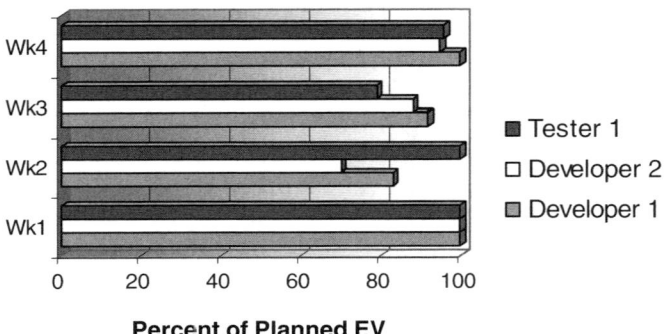

Figure 5-23 ● Team-level Earned Value

the previous releases were a week late, it's a good bet this one will be a week late too. If they hit their targets, this one probably will too.

The more direct answer is to look at team-level earned value. If the defect rate in the current release is having an impact, it will be noticed more easily at the individual resource level. Using team earned value will also allow you to corroborate the direct and indirect approach findings.

The data for the first four weeks of the release cycle is shown in Figure 5-23. There's a drop in productivity in Weeks 2 and 3, which corresponds to the spike in defects in the rate in Figure 5-20. In Week 4, the actual earned value tracks close to plan. The best answer to the third question about the impact on other tasks is that although it is too early to tell if other project work will be impacted, the current data suggests it will not.

● APPLYING WHAT YOU'VE LEARNED

You've been shown a number of puzzle pieces in the previous sections. You've also seen how some of those pieces fit together to form the larger picture of project performance. The first two exercises here will give you some practice in interpreting the indicators.

The third exercise requires you to look at the puzzle as a whole, tying together the measures of the last three chapters with the architectural aspects presented in Chapter 2.

Exercise 5-1: Historical Data Comparisons

Be wary of comparisons of historical data where the environmental factors are dissimilar. Factors such as time allocated to requirements specification or test, the complexity of the proposed solution, or even changes in personnel can affect schedule performance and defect rates. For example, suppose we compare defect incidence for two projects: a maintenance effort and a new development effort. Figure 5-24 shows the results of the comparison for the same period of time.

On the face of it, the maintenance project has a lower defect rate than the new development effort. This seems reasonable, since new development tends to generate more defects than updating the product for a new platform or adding some customer-requested enhancements. But is this really a legitimate comparison? Why or why not?

Exercise 5-2: Using Defect Rates and Attributes

Suppose you have been selected to be the project manager for the next functional release of a web-based application that provides

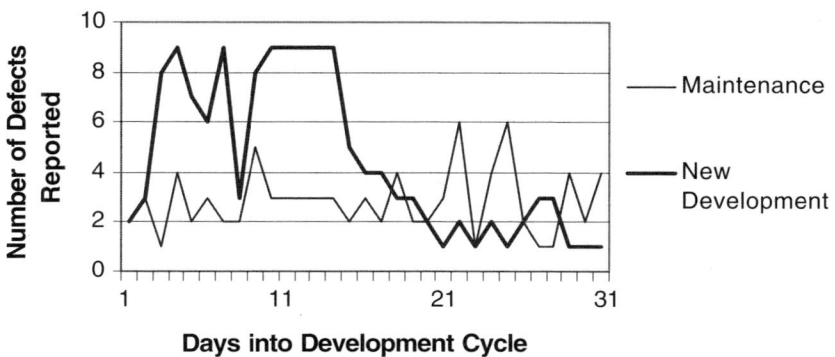

Figure 5-24 ■ Comparing Historical Defect Rates

relocation information and services for the general web-viewing public. These services include collecting, comparing, and displaying data from moving companies, realty firms, and government repositories of census data, crime statistics, etc. The previous release has not been altogether successful. While the hit rate on the web site has remained high, users have logged many problem reports on the application since its first release.

The only data you have for the previous release is two charts, shown in Figures 5-25 and 5-26. Based on this information, answer the following questions:

1. What appears to have gone wrong in the first development effort?
2. Does the increase in requirements defects in the acceptance test phase provide a clue to the high defect rates since product release?
3. Does the rejected-reports rate support or challenge your answer to question 2?
4. Based on these charts, what risks do you face in the second development effort?

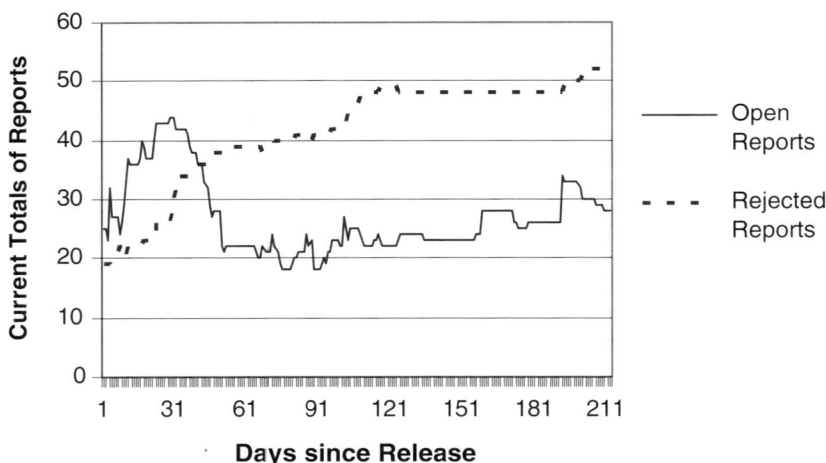

Figure 5-25 ■ Previous Release's Post-shipment Defect Rate

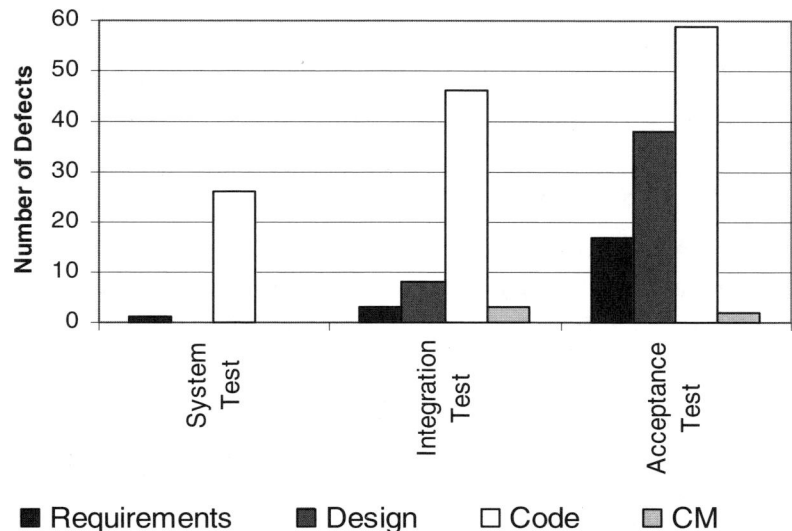

■ Requirements   ■ Design   □ Code   ▨ CM

Figure 5-26 ● Previous Release's Pre-shipment Injection and Detection Phase Data

5. What steps will you take to mitigate these risks in your project?

Exercise 5-3: Creating a Measurement Specification

Now that you understand the concepts of measurement architecture, measures, and indicators, it is time to apply that knowledge to a measurement specification. The specification serves several purposes:

- It is a record of your rationale for implementing the measures you chose.
- It describes the relationships between base measures, derived measures, and indicators.
- It provides interpretation guidelines.
- It is a resource for training others in how to generate and use the measures.
- It is a required work product for some software development standards and quality management systems.

One possible format for a measurement specification is shown in Figure 5-27. This format combines features of the specification formats presented in IEEE 1061-1998, *Standard for a Software Quality Metrics Methodology*, and ISO/IEC 15939:2002, *Software engineering – Software measurement process.* Figure 5-28 illustrates how to complete the form using the example of defect containment.

Using this format (or something of your own choosing), create at least three specification tables that describe your measures. If you have trouble with the form at first, it may be because you are having trouble defining the measure from its strategic position "downward" to its base measures. In this case, start by defining your base measures and work "upward" in the architecture, addressing derived measures, then indicators, and then finally the strategic use of the measurement.

<name of the measurement>	
Strategic Value	
Information Need	<the issue related to this measure; the problem that the measure helps solve; the management responsibility that the measure supports>
Measurable Concept	<the significance of the function or aspect that will be measured; the business goal or value that this measure supports>
Relevant Entities	<processes, products, components, work products, etc. that will be targeted by the measure>
Attributes	<specific aspects or parts of the entities that will be measured>
Costs	<cost of collecting, calculating, interpreting, and reporting this measure>
Benefits	<the insight this measure will provide with respect to business goals; how this measure will satisfy the information need; why this measure is better than an alternative measure>
Impact	<how the measurable concept relates to business goals and/or to operations; how it can be used in decisions about products and processes>
Implementation	
Base Measure(s)	<the attributes, units, and scale of the base measure(s) being used>
Measurement Method(s)	<time and place and responsible individual(s) required for this measurement>
Type of Measurement	<incidence, diagnostic, heuristic>
Derived Measure(s)	<the derived measure(s) related to the base measure(s)>
Computation	<how to calculate the derived measure(s)>
Interpretation	<guidelines for interpretation of the results of the derived measure(s)>
Indicator	<the indicator(s) that will be generated from the derived measure(s)>
Model	<the calculations required to create the indicator(s) from the derived measure(s)>
Decision Criteria	<the significance of the indicator(s) and guidelines for interpreting and acting upon the value of indicator(s)>

Figure 5-27 ● Measurement Specification Form Adapted from IEEE 1061-1998 and ISO/IEC 15939:2002

Service Call Avoidance – Software Defects	
Strategic Value	
Information Need	How effective are we at keeping defects from the installed base?
Measurable Concept	Defect Containment
Relevant Entities	• Problem reports generated during development. • Problem reports generated after shipment by field service and customers.
Attributes	• Detection Phase field in problem reports in the problem report tracking system. • Customer-perceived severity rating of the problem reports filed by field service or customer.
Costs	Monthly data collection and reporting are already accounted for in the administrative budget for department XYZ.
Benefits	Problem reports from the field are a direct, quantitative measurement of software product performance and can be correlated with development processes more directly than customer satisfaction surveys or interviews.
Impact	• Defects released to the installed base directly affect customer perceptions of product quality. • A high incidence of defect remediation can result in increased service costs and a decrease in the margin for maintenance agreements. • Trends in defect containment should be used to evaluate development processes.
Implementation	
Base Measure(s)	• Number of defects reported by development during development phase, of any severity, per release. • Number of defects reported by field service or customer, of any severity higher than inconvenience, per release.
Measurement Method(s)	Specific query in problem reporting tool.
Type of Measurement	Incidence.
Derived Measure(s)	Percentage of total known defects contained before shipment.
DM Computation	Number of defects reported by development during development phase/(Total known defects in reporting system for a release – Total known defects reported by field service or customer assigned an "inconvenience" severity level), expressed as a percentage.
Interpretation	Derived measure will indicate 100% containment at release date, but should track downward over time. If no downward trend is evident, verify installation dates and investigate customer usage rates to determine if lack of trend is due to lack of use or to high product quality.
Indicator	Containment Trend Line, monthly data points for six months after release.
Model	Six consecutive DM computations plotted against time.
Decision Criteria	Number of defects discovered by field service or customer should not exceed 5% of the total number of defects discovered by development prior to release.

Figure 5-28 ■ Measurement Specification Form for Defect Containment

Graphical Display of Data

What is a good chart? The simplest answer is: one that tells a story. You should have a point to make through the data, and you should make that point efficiently. If you have structured your measurement effort properly, you shouldn't have any trouble determining what your point is; the derived measures and the indicators should say it all for you. As for getting that point across efficiently, that often calls for some experimentation. Some chart formats work better than others for different types of stories.

● GUIDELINES FOR COMMON GRAPH TYPES

There are no universal rules for graphics, but management consultants, technical writers, and academics seem to be in agreement about the best uses for some of the simpler charting formats.

Data Tables

Tables are useful graphical aids only when the audience needs to see the detailed, numerical data. In most cases you will want to create charts that individually highlight one or more aspects of the data.

	Release X.1	Release X.2	Release X.3
Reviews	4	2	
Unit Testing	8	1	
System Testing	61	13	8
Acceptance Testing	4	4	1
Warranty	12	2	

Figure 6-1 ● Data for Release X

With small amounts of data, you can always generate a chart that includes the data in tabular form. The original data table is shown in Figure 6-1, while Figure 6-2 shows the data charted as a bar graph with the tabular data attached. This approach is useful when the data covers a wide range (as it does in this example). In the chart, the smaller data points like "reviews" are dwarfed by the larger data points like "system testing." Including the data table lets

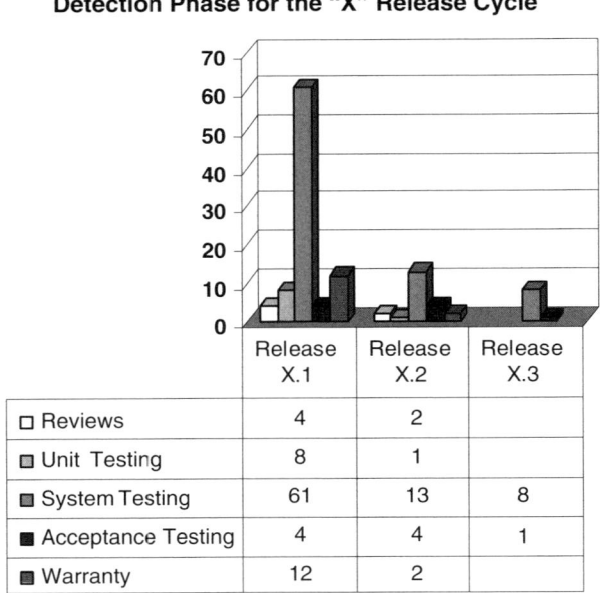

Detection Phase for the "X" Release Cycle

	Release X.1	Release X.2	Release X.3
☐ Reviews	4	2	
▨ Unit Testing	8	1	
▨ System Testing	61	13	8
■ Acceptance Testing	4	4	1
▨ Warranty	12	2	

Figure 6-2 ● Bar Chart with Data Table

your audience see what the actual data is for the comparatively small columns on the graph.

Line Charts

Line charts or trend or run rate charts are used for showing changes in one or more attributes over time. When charting more than one attribute, make sure that the attributes all have the same scale, lie within the same relative range, and have the same significance within that range. The chart in Figure 6-3 is hard to read because one of the attributes, "reopen," doesn't lie in the same range as the other two attributes, "open" and "new."

Whenever possible, make sure that all attributes are analyzed as run rates. Do not mix complete run rate data with partial incidence data on the same chart. The chart in Figure 6-4 is hard to follow because the number of defects discovered appears as tally points while the other data is run data.

Bar Charts

Bar charts are used to highlight comparisons of one or more attributes across some category or at discrete points in time. In Fig-

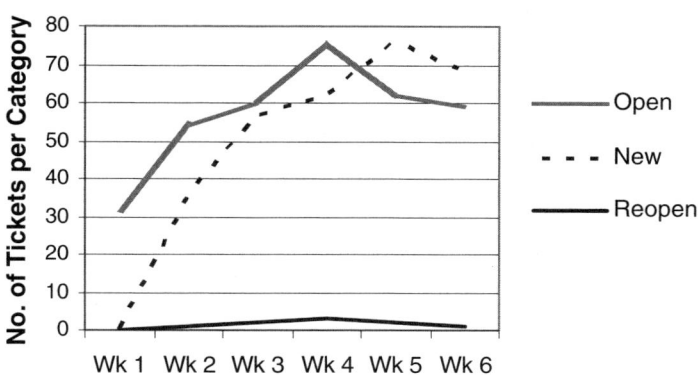

Figure 6-3 ● Mismatched Data Ranges

Desktop Review Hours and Defects

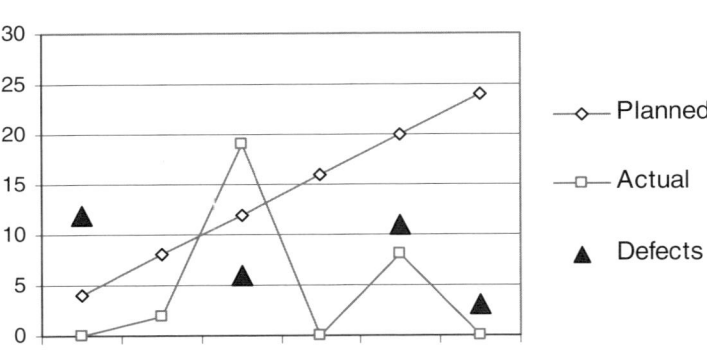

Figure 6-4 ● Partial Incidence Data

ure 6-5, vertical bars are used to show the total number of defects per root-cause category for each sample date. Since the sampling is roughly periodic, the chart also shows something about overall trending.

One typical problem with bar charts is the sequence of the data series. When you load raw data into a spreadsheet, it is likely to be

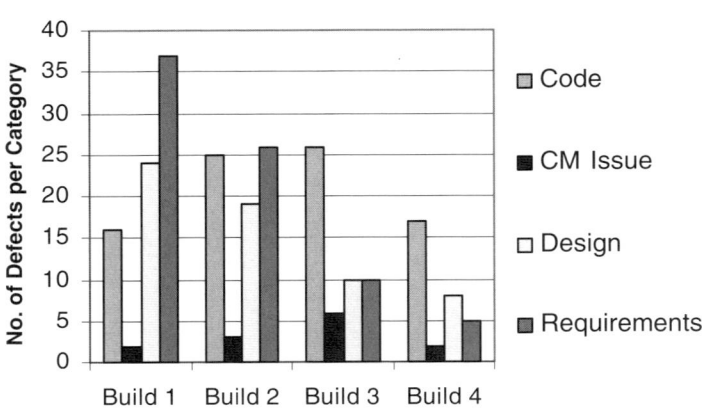

Figure 6-5 ● Root Cause Displayed as Simple Bar Chart

in a sequence determined by the query you used. When you chart it, it may not tell the story as well as you would like it to. In Figure 6-5, if your tale is the increase in code-related defects over time, the chart is fine. If you wanted to highlight the increase in both code- and software design-related defects over time, you would want to rearrange the data in the columns so that the software design data is next to the code data.

Bars can be stacked for comparative contribution. Numerical stacked bars are best used when the values of the components being stacked are similar (otherwise you end up with a few thick layers and some very thin ones). Percentage stacked bars should be used to show percentage of total count across the category, not the relative percentage of some attributes in that category.

Figure 6-6 uses the same data as Figure 6-5, but the data is displayed using a percent stacked bar. This approach emphasizes the relative contribution of each type of root cause for each sample date. The size of each slice across the sample dates can be used to show trending (keeping in mind that these trends are relative percentages).

A bar chart isn't appropriate in some cases. If there's one data point with a very high value compared to the other data points, it

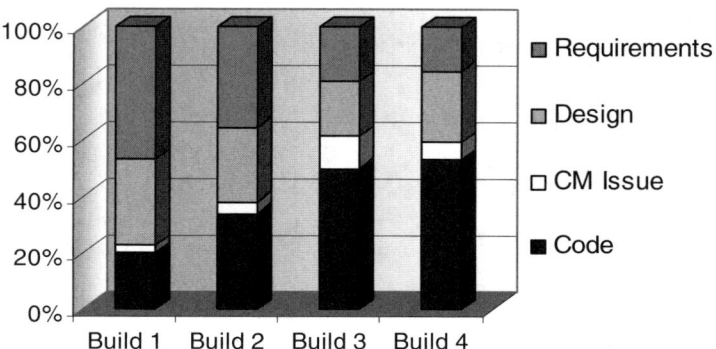

Figure 6-6 ● Root Cause Displayed as Stacked Bar Chart

will cause your chart to be imbalanced. Figure 6-7 illustrates this problem. The chart makes it clear that "system test" found most of the defects in the release. However, it takes a little effort to determine the significance of the data for the other phases because the bars are truncated.

If you were the system test manager, this chart might be perfectly acceptable, since it easily tells the story of how your team saved the release from certain disaster. If you were the SQA manager trying to impress upon senior managers the need to beef up unit testing, this imbalanced chart might help you make that point. As a record of phase containment, however, it is not particularly easy to read. For this, a percent stacked bar might be a better choice (see Figure 6-8).

When the data includes both positive and negative values with a wide range, the percent stacked bar chart won't solve the problem. You will either have to find a way to group the data into similar ranges or just accept the disparity in bar heights (or depths). Also remember that negative values carry negative connotations. If a negative value is good news (e.g., when the project team comes in under budget), you might want to consider ways to present this as a positive value rather than a negative one.

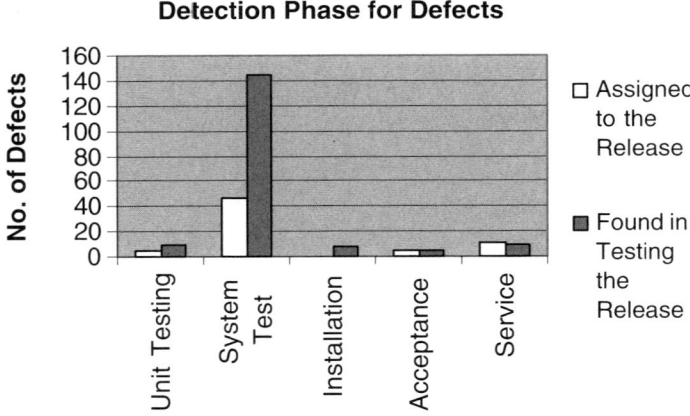

Figure 6-7 ● Imbalanced Data

Detection Phase for Defects

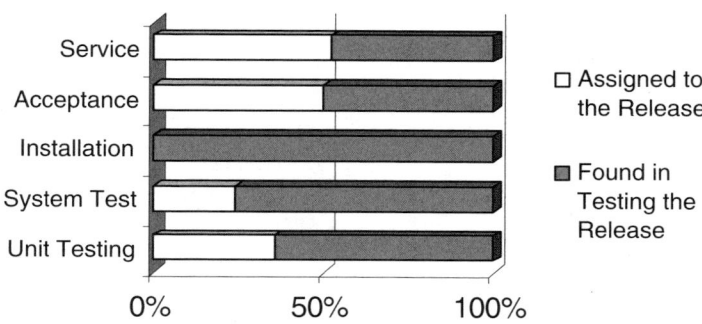

Figure 6-8 ● Correcting Imbalance with Percent Stacked Bars

Pie Charts

The pie chart displays the percentage or numerical contribution of attributes within one category or for one sample time period. The pie should have no more than seven sections (some say no more than five). The pie should display the information clockwise from largest contribution to smallest contribution.

The chart in Figure 6-9 uses the same data as the bar charts did. But the pie chart has to be focused on a single sample date and the

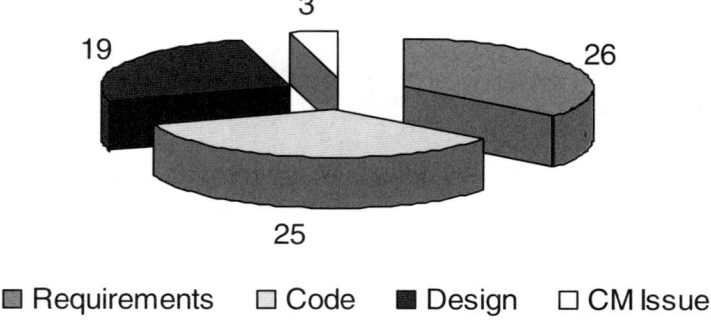

Figure 6-9 ● Root Cause Displayed as Pie Chart

data has to be rearranged to comply with the pie chart display sequence guidelines.

Area Charts

Stacked line or area charts can be used instead of stacked (numerical) bar charts when the contribution over time is important and the time needs to be displayed as continuous. One of the benefits of an area chart is that it uses a lot of space to highlight comparative contributions. One of its main disadvantages is that if the values include both very large and very small values, the smaller values are easily lost in the graph. Figure 6-10 is an example of an area chart for problem reports by state and sampling date.

Generally, the area chart should focus on one attribute; if two or more attributes are used, they should have the same unit of measure. Figure 6-11 presents the defect rate and the mean time to fix a defect for several components. The chart is a poor use of the area chart because the values being presented are not the same: mean time to fix a defect is measured in hours, and defects are measured as numerical counts. Some of the key points of this data get lost in this presentation. In particular, the mean time to fix defects in Component D is four hours, but the significance of this may be lost because the defect count is so low (one).

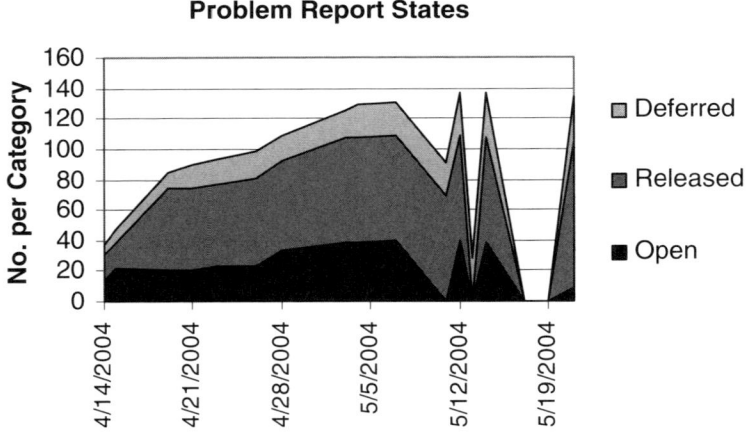

Figure 6-10 ■ Stacked Area Chart

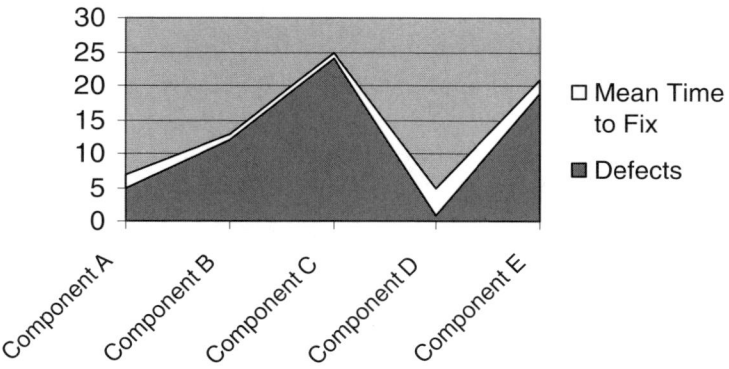

Figure 6-11 ● Mixed Units of Measure

Even with the same attribute, we need to be wary of the scale in an area chart. The chart in Figure 6-12 compares mean time to fix defects in several components across two releases. The areas displayed are large enough to make an impact, and the graph uses a single unit of measure—hours on the Y axis. The problem is that the area chart "stacks" its values. So while mean time to fix for Component D actually decreased by .7 hours between Release 1 and Release 2, it's quite easy to misinterpret the graph and think that the mean time to fix for Component D is more than seven hours.

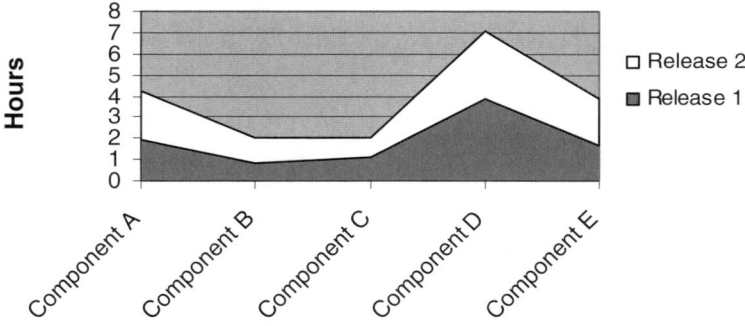

Figure 6-12 ● Potential Pitfall of Stacking Data

To avoid the stacking effect, we can use an Area-Bar chart (see Figure 6-13). The chart is based on the same data as the chart in Figure 6-12 but it is easier to understand and it also has a more granular scale on the Y axis.

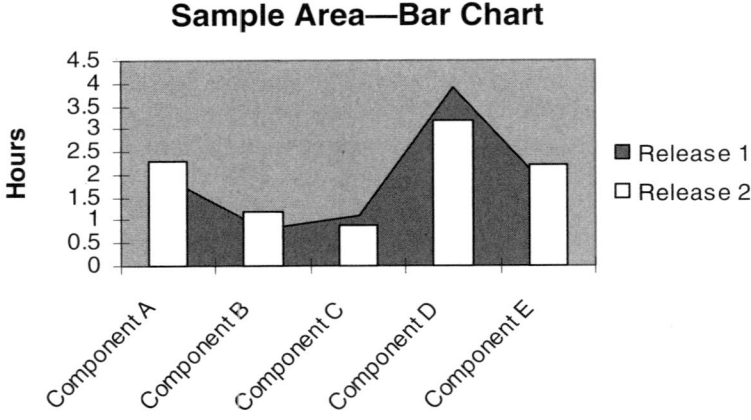

Figure 6-13 ● Correcting Problem of Stacking

● GRAPHICAL PITFALLS

The classic texts in graphical design were written before we all became accustomed to how spreadsheet and statistical software packages display data in charts. Purists may lament the passing of the era of pure black-and-white or hand-drawn charts. We can still learn a few lessons from that early research, however.

Focus and Vibration

A graphic should reveal the significance of the data, not call attention to itself. When we want to emphasize or highlight some aspect of the data, we often resort to graphical techniques that can divert viewer attention away from the data toward the design.

The black-and-white area chart in Figure 6-14 was intended to call attention to Component C's high defect rate. The problem is, it doesn't do that. The contrast between dark and light calls attention to

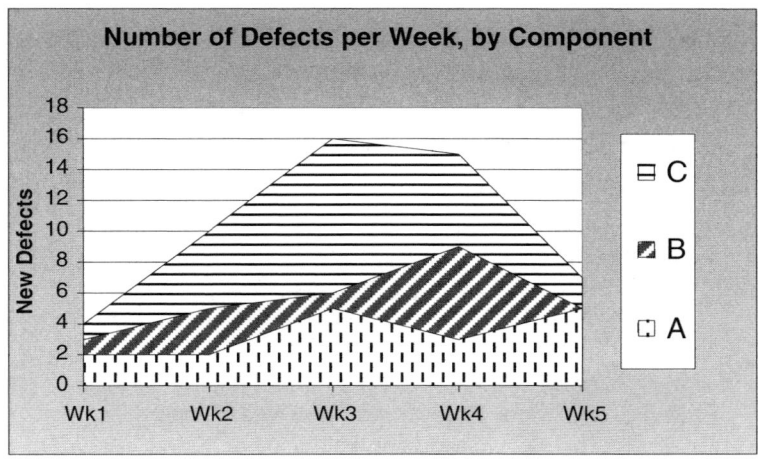

Figure 6-14 ● Contrast and Vibration

Component B's area, not to Component C. Further, the patterns used are jarring to the eye: stare long enough at Component C's area and you'll experience the optical illusion of "vibration" in the graphic.

You can get the same message across by using grey shades and ordering the columns so that the most important column is on the left. In the example in Figure 6-15, grid lines were added but the line color was changed to white to mute the effect on the vertical bars.

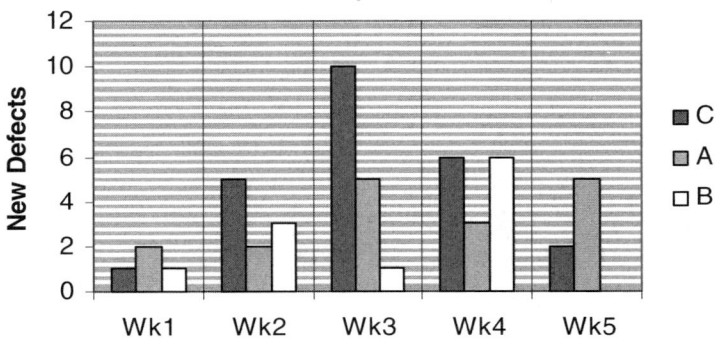

Figure 6-15 ● Correcting Problem of Vibration and Contrast

Details and Clutter

Despite your best attempt to put the story into the picture and leave the data behind, someone is going to ask you for the numbers themselves. Percent stacked bar charts are a case in point. Percent stacked bar charts tell stories about comparative value or weighting; the message is in the relative amounts of shading in the column. Invariably, someone wants to know what the actual numbers were. Obligingly, you add them (see Figure 6-16).

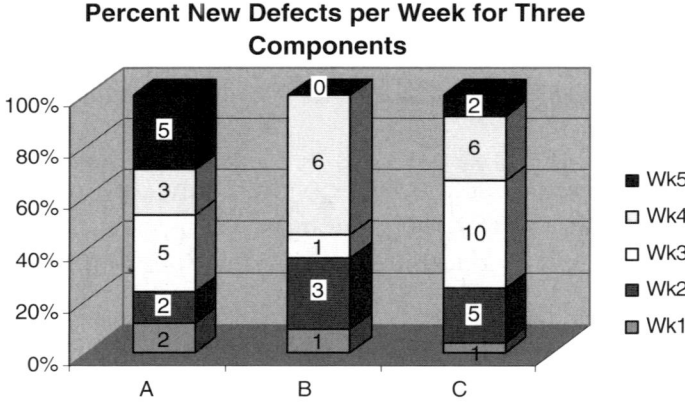

Figure 6-16 ● Clarity or Clutter?

Now you have clutter. Not only do the numbers conflict with the graph's scale of percentages, but they cause more design problems. The numbers for Week 5 were originally in black and were invisible. The Week 2 values were visible but barely readable. If you change their format background, you introduce another diversion with the white blocks. You could spend your afternoon dragging the value objects around the graph, changing their font size, etc., or you could just graph the numerical values in another, non-stacked chart.

Fonts, Weights, and Patterns

If you have designed your graph properly, it should tell its story without additional emphasis from font changes, line weights, or patterns. For example, a standard Microsoft Excel bar chart already has several design elements that convey the significance of the data. The bars have a certain height and width, are colored, etc. Adding any embellishments is likely to detract from the message.

Some embellishments are just noise. Others can border on the tasteless. Figure 6-17 includes examples of both. Adding the bold italic font setting to the labels on the X and Y axes doesn't provide any additional information; it just draws attention to the labels instead of the graph. Using different colors, patterns, and line weights to highlight the differences between the components is at best redundant, and at worst just plain ugly.

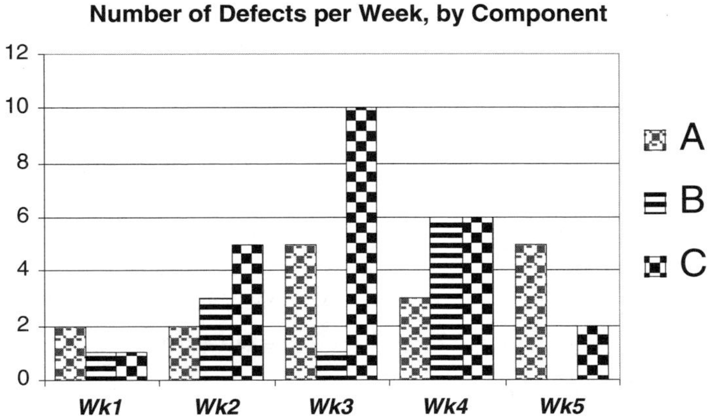

Figure 6-17 ● Over-the-Top Embellishment

● APPLYING WHAT YOU'VE LEARNED

Exercise 6-1: Release Profile

Based on the material in this and previous chapters, you are now well prepared to lay out a scorecard for your software projects. To avoid any confusion with a PMO level scorecard, we'll refer to this report as a release profile.

Your profile should be all graphics or at least include minimal text. In other words, the graphics have to tell the story on their own. Depending on your corporate culture, you may be expected to follow some standard format (all line charts, all bar charts, etc.). If you have your choice of format, it is generally helpful to vary the type of chart used. This not only gives you more freedom in how you get your points across, but it is also less tedious for the viewer.

Figures 6-18 through 6-21 show the graphics for a "four-up" profile. Study those charts and then answer the following questions:

1. Why do you think these measures were chosen for the profile?
2. What measures would you have chosen for the profile?
3. What do these charts tell you about the current release?
4. Do the graphics illustrate any of the graphic pitfalls discussed in this chapter?

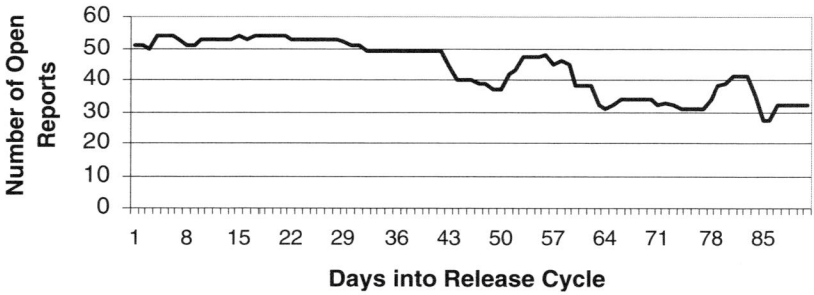

Figure 6-18 ● Profile Open Run Rate

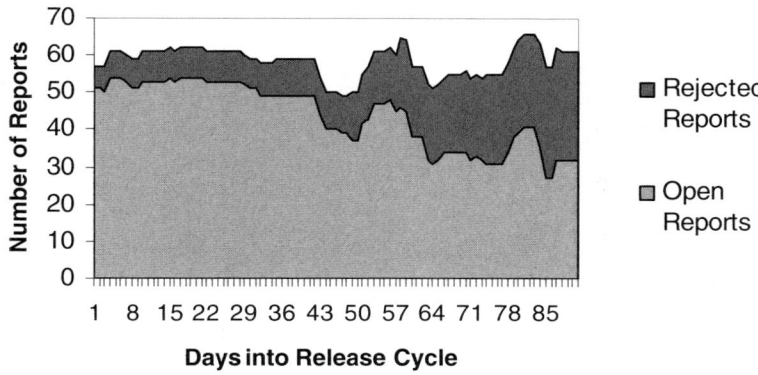

Figure 6-19 ● Profile Open vs. Rejected Comparison

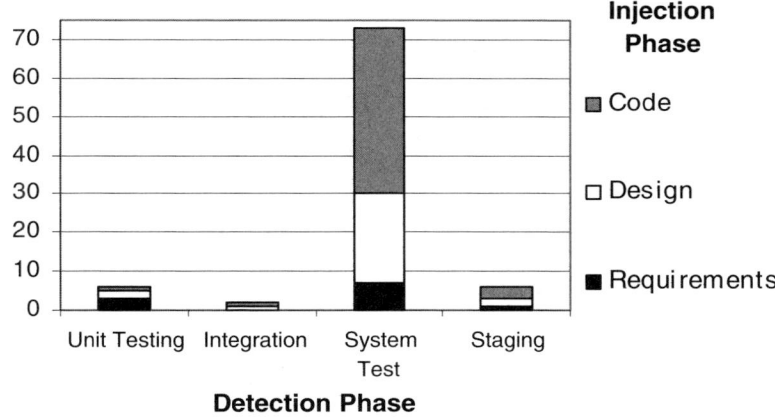

Figure 6-20 ● Profile Injection and Detection Phase Data

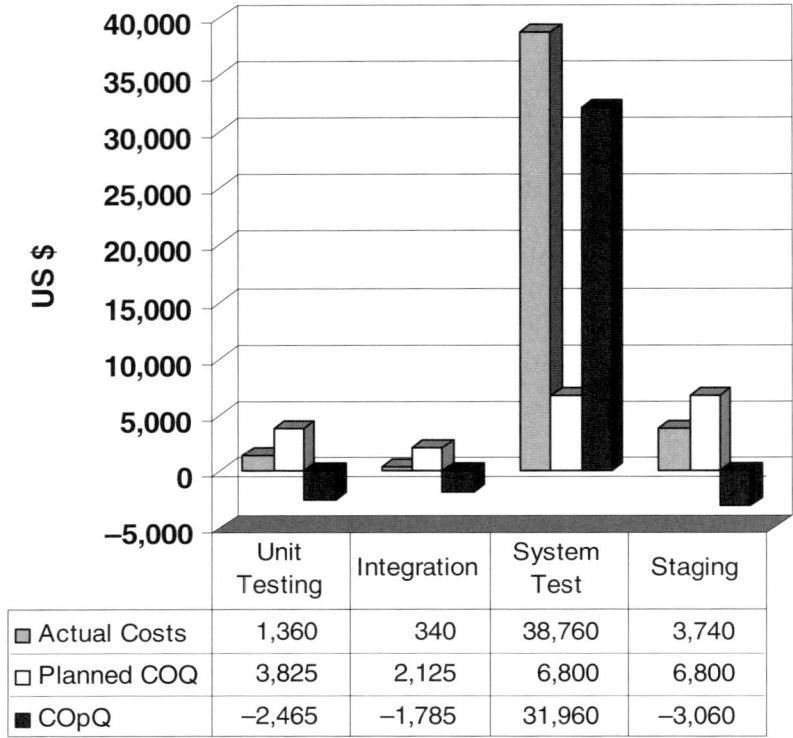

	Unit Testing	Integration	System Test	Staging
▨ Actual Costs	1,360	340	38,760	3,740
☐ Planned COQ	3,825	2,125	6,800	6,800
■ COpQ	−2,465	−1,785	31,960	−3,060

Figure 6-21 ● Profile COQ/COpQ

CHAPTER

7

Reality Check: The Human Side of the Numbers

In Chapter 1 I remarked that you can't worry about maturity levels when you are constantly living on the edge of crises. I'm sure you have found a few tricks and techniques since then that will help you back away from the edge and perhaps avoid it altogether. But there is more to measurement than querying defect databases and parsing timesheets into cost categories. There's the human side of the numbers, which includes using measurement to improve the work environment as well as using information about your team's behavior patterns to help interpret the data.

In previous chapters, the examples of how to apply measurement were simply expositions: Here's the situation and here's how to analyze it using these measures. We'll take that approach just twice more in the first two sections of this chapter when we look at deferral rates and ship readiness. When it comes to improving the work environment, however, the issues are more managerial than technical. I might even say that the issues are ethical too.

It seems inappropriate to present that kind of material in bulleted lists of dos and don'ts and process steps. So most of this chapter is devoted to short vignettes that illustrate how measurement data can be used to benefit your team and co-workers. Not quite case studies and not quite pure fiction, these narratives are based on actual situations, with appropriate precautions taken to protect the people and data originally involved.

■ NO NEWS ISN'T ALWAYS GOOD NEWS

While Change Control Boards are intended to manage changes to a product, they can also become a bottleneck and slow down the release. Like any group of individuals, CCB members have their own priorities and agendas; it is important to monitor change activity to ensure that necessary changes are being made rather than postponed.

Figure 7-1 is an area chart showing, for a period of 23 days, the number of problem reports that the CCB dispatched to one of three states:

- *Deferred.* The fix for the defect has been scheduled into a future release.

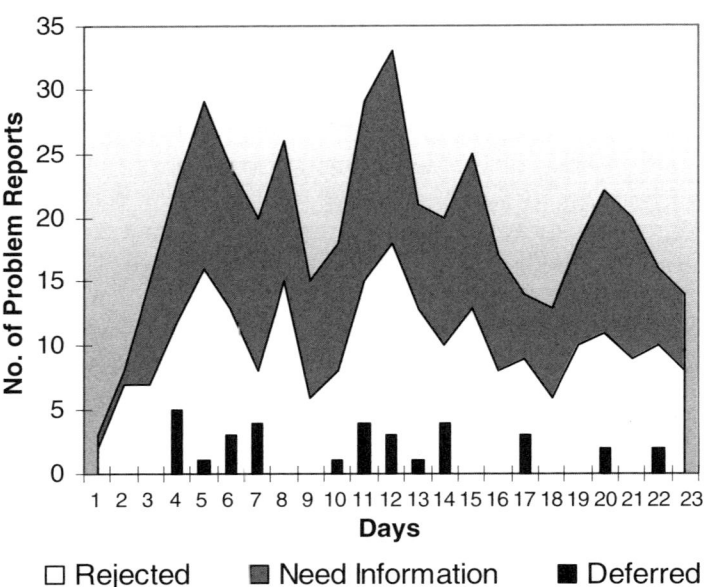

Change Control Board Actions

Figure 7-1 ■ Current Run Rates for CCB Activity

- *Need information.* The report has been sent back to the testing or support or engineering group for clarification.
- *Rejected.* The report has been closed because the problem could not be reproduced or was not considered to be a legitimate problem.

In the change control system reflected in this graph, assigning any one of these state values to the problem report removes it from consideration for the current release. Deferred problem reports are moved out to a future release. Rejected reports are no longer active at all. Need-information reports will return to the CCB after the information has been added, at which time the CCB may then open them to be fixed in the current release, reject them, or defer them.

One can imagine that, as the release effort nears its scheduled end date, there is substantial pressure on the CCB to move reports to one of these states so they will not adversely impact the current release date. It is clear from Figure 7-1 that need-information and rejected reports account for the majority of the states, and there are comparatively few deferred reports. On the face of it, the release seems to be having no significant problems.

But a trend like this should alert the project manager that there may be something seriously wrong in the release. Why? If the reports had all the necessary information and were actual defects, the CCB would have been able to open them rather than move them to "need information." That category is used when the report does not fully explain the nature of the problem and/or does not fully justify why this is a problem. "Need information" indicates one of two possibilities:

1. The reports were improperly or inadequately filled out.
2. The functionality of the release content is poorly defined and there's disagreement about what the product should (or should not) do under certain circumstances.

Assuming that the folks reporting the problems were adequately trained in the report tool and knew how to describe problems properly, the only alternative is to assume that release functionality was, at least in these cases, ambiguously defined. The number of rejected reports seems to corroborate this assumption, since reports can be rejected because they are deemed to be spurious problems.

Let's assume that builds were dropped to the test team on days 1, 9, and 18. Days 9 and 18 show a trough followed by a peak. We can safely assume that the troughs are due to installing the new build and setting up for the test runs. Now look at the rejected incidence in relation to the builds. In both the first and second builds, there's a jump in the number of problems reported that the CCB deemed to be spurious. This is odd. The test team should be fully aware of the release requirements, the intended scope of functionality, and so forth.

Late in a release, a test team might stretch its testing into components and functions that aren't essential to the release, just to "push the envelope." This type of testing might well generate reports that the CCB thought should be deferred or maybe rejected. Early in a release, however, these status rates probably indicate a problem with requirements and a high maintenance load after the release. After all, if the engineering and test groups aren't sure how the product should behave, how likely is it that the customer will be satisfied with that behavior?

Ideally, the project manager would be able to corroborate his or her interpretation of the CCB activity with data on the type of testing that generated the problem reports. Figure 7-2 shows an example of such data collected for four types of testing: installation, testing of new functionality, compatibility testing across several different platforms, and stress testing. For the same time period in the release, tests directed at new functionality generated the majority of the defects. This supports the diagnosis that the product has significant requirement issues. It's probably time for a thorough review of the requirements and design with both the account team and the customer.

● ARE WE READY TO SHIP?

You can draw some reasonable conclusions about project risks when you understand how long your find-fix-retest cycle takes and

Relative Percent of Test Failures

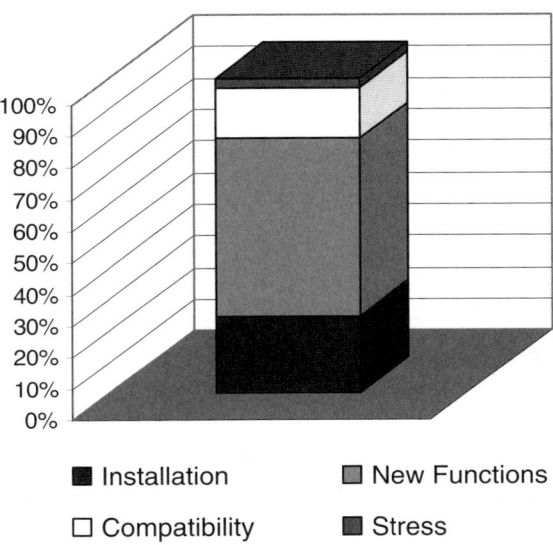

■ Installation   ■ New Functions

☐ Compatibility   ■ Stress

Figure 7-2 ● Types of Tests that Failed in the Same Period

how effective it is. Combining this information with the number of defects you have to fix, you can estimate how much project time will be used up in maintenance. This can be especially helpful in the last few weeks of a project, when there are still lots of defects to fix and your boss is suffering from a bad case of ship anxiety.

Typically, some of the defects reported early in a release cycle will not be fixed until later in the cycle. This is fine as long as it doesn't create such a large backlog that either development or test can't work through the backlog by the scheduled release date. A graph like the one in Figure 7-3 can be helpful in determining whether the backlog is being reduced in a timely fashion.

This chart tracks both the number of defect reports assigned to each build and the number of defects that are still open in subsequent weeks. In Figure 7-3, Build 3 occurs in Week 3 and has 19 defects initially assigned to it. By Week 4, there are 11 open defects

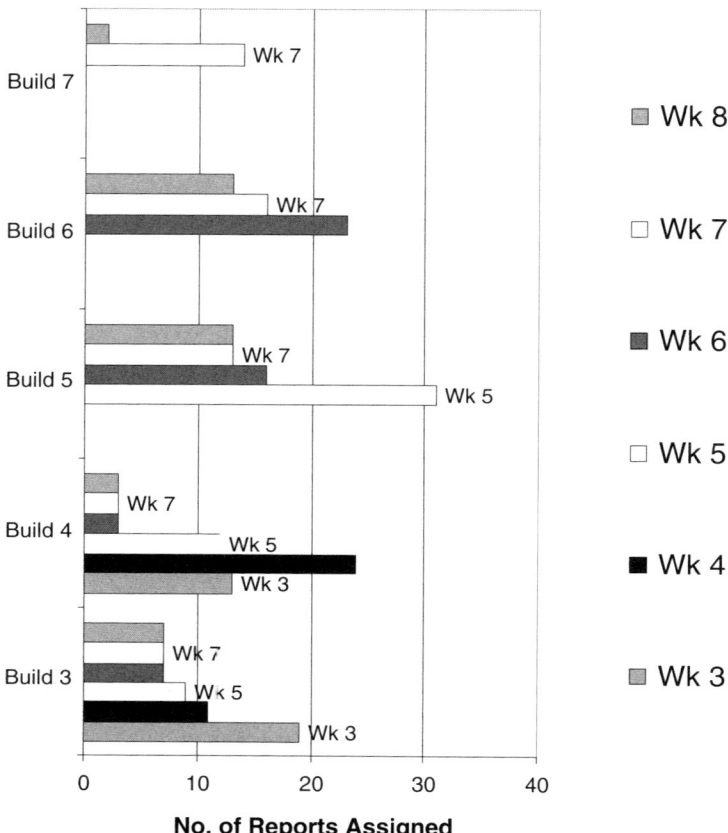

Figure 7-3 ● Build Assignment Rates

originating in Build 3. In Week 5, there are 9. Build 4, occurring in Week 4, inherits many open defects from Build 3.

A chart such as this is not to be used for presenting data to stakeholders because it combines so many factors and is hard to read. As an analysis tool, however, it can help you quickly identify peaks in the work load late in the cycle. Without knowing anything about the development cycle, it is clear from this chart that later builds started with a high number of assigned defects. The values for Build 4, Build 5, and Build 6 in Weeks 5 through 7 show that late in the development cycle the project team was still struggling with a high number of defect reports.

In practice, the chart in Figure 7-3 would be updated weekly from some baseline date. The data presented would be used to help answer two questions:

➤ Are these peaks due to poor quality; that is, are we finding an unusually high number of defects? Or are these peaks due to defect fixes being deferred until a later build?

➤ Will we be ready to ship?

Normally, a team will use this chart and a line chart showing new defect detection rates per build to help it answer the first question. We'll ignore the discovery rate data for a moment because I want to show how it is possible to answer the first question from the assignment data alone. For the discussion that follows, assume that builds are done weekly and the current assignment tallies are made just prior to the build. Assume also that if a defect is fixed in a release, it remains assigned to that release.

The baseline for this example was made in Week 3 when Build 3 was performed. In Week 3, defects are already being deferred to Build 4 (see Figure 7-4).

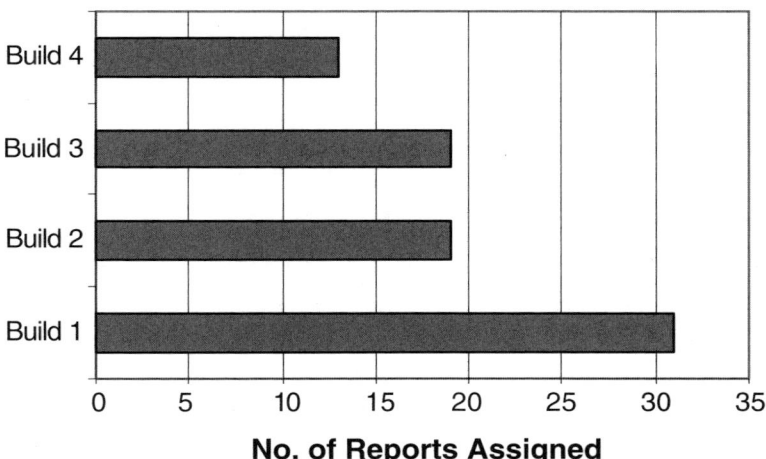

No. of Reports Assigned

Figure 7-4 ● Week 3 Data

By Week 5, the situation has worsened. As the chart in Figure 7-5 shows, Build 4 had a high number of defects assigned to it in Week 4. Were these fixed or deferred? They were not fixed—the data for Build 4 in Week 5 shows very few reports. That means that most of the reports were reassigned to Build 5.

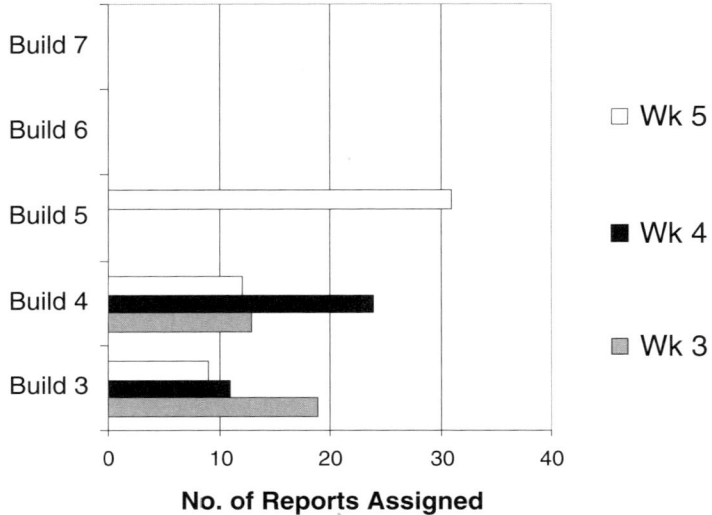

Figure 7-5 ● Data for Weeks 3 through 5

By Week 6, there's good news and bad news, as Figure 7-6 shows.

Comparing the Week 5 and Week 6 bars for Build 5, we can see that by Build 6, the development and test teams were able to reduce the backlog of defects by 50 percent. That's the good news. But a significant number of defects must still be fixed before the release can ship. Further, looking at the decreasing tally for Build 3 in Week 4, Week 5, and Week 6, we can see that the development team is still fixing defects from the third build! That's the bad news: The project is still at risk from decisions about deferrals made several weeks ago.

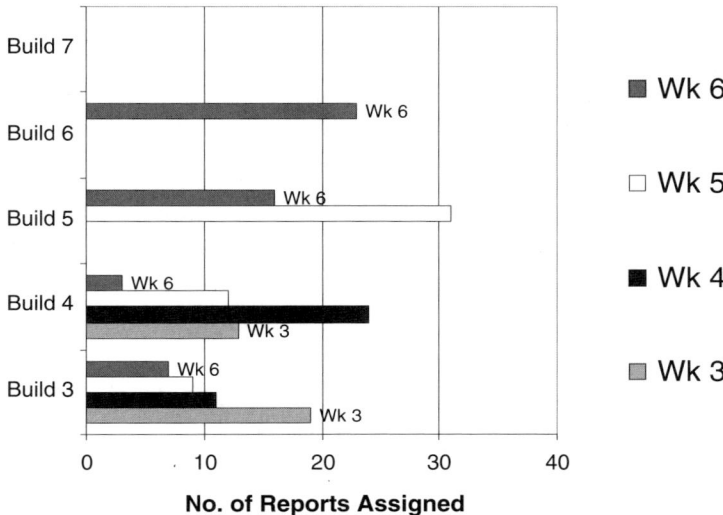

Figure 7-6 ● Data for Weeks 3 through 6

The point here is that this kind of data can be used to understand the level of risk to the project even without supplemental data from other sources. High deferral rates early on or in the middle of the project may help the team meet the immediate build dates, but the price later in the cycle may be high. There's also a lesson here for future projects: Deferrals should be made judiciously with an eye toward the impact on the weeks of the project.

All lessons aside, suppose the ship date is in Week 8. Will the product be ready to ship? Based on the data above, the project team has every good reason to fear they will not be able to ship on time. With a large backlog, the risk of schedule slips is high. Every code change carries with it the risk that it will destabilize some part of the code, maybe even some other fix checked in at the same time. The risk increases as more changes are made.

Many development and project managers think assigning overtime to work through such a backlog is the solution, but such a solution addresses the wrong problem. It's not the workload that needs to be managed; it's the risk to product integrity within that workload that must be managed. Even if the workload *per se* were the key problem, overtime can be counterproductive: harried, tired developers and testers make more mistakes than those who are not under such pressure. What we need here is an analysis based on risk, not effort. That will require more information.

It is now Week 7, and the situation appears gloomy (see Figure 7-7). Fourteen defects are assigned into Build 7, with one week to go before shipment. Can the project team make it?

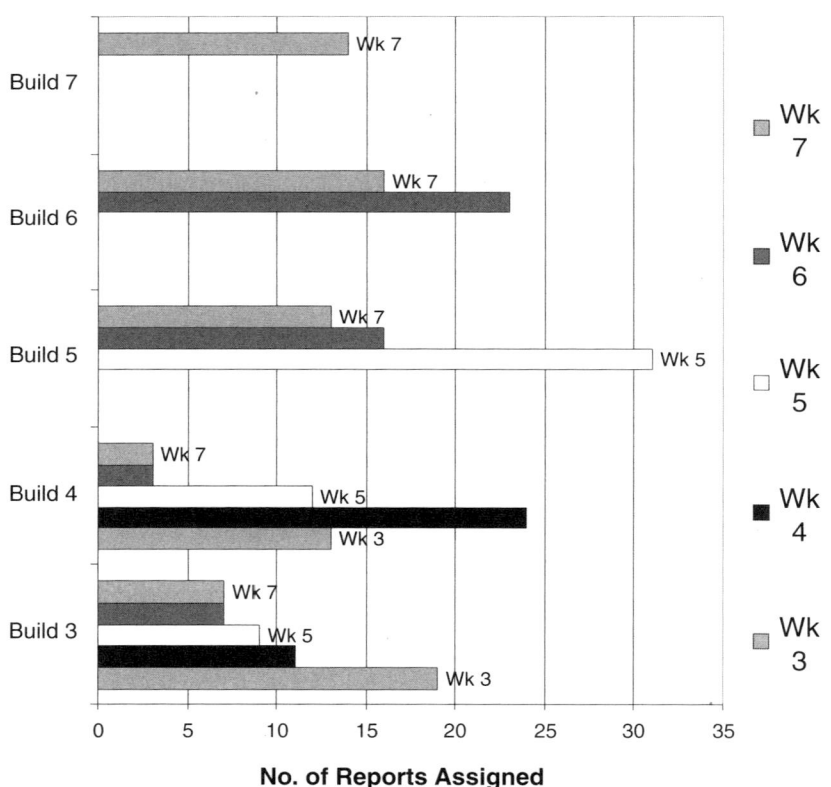

No. of Reports Assigned

Figure 7-7 ● Data up to Week 7

The answer depends on the ship criteria, of course. If the test team needs two weeks to test the final build, then there's not enough time in the schedule. If the ship criteria state that the test team simply has to validate any new fixes before shipment, then there's a chance the product can meet its date. Let's assume that the project only has to meet the latter requirement.

The project team can use other data to determine the likelihood of making the date. If the project has been tracking Change Control Board activity and defect report states, it will be possible to determine the run rates and averages for several key factors. Suppose for the sake of illustration that the historical data shows that if the fixes are good, the test team can close on average nine problem reports per day. So if Build 7 has only 14 defect fixes to test, the workload is reasonable within the time left on the project. The only risks left are new defects and bad fixes.

Based on project data for new defects discovered in the last couple of weeks (see Figure 7-8), there's a low risk of finding new defects. Although the linear trend is not at zero, no defects have been discovered in the past few days.

The other risk is bad fixes. The development team has intermittently been making mistakes when it fixed defects. As Figure 7-9 shows, these "bad fixes" are low in number, and none of them has occurred in the last week despite the added pressure on the development team to meet the date.

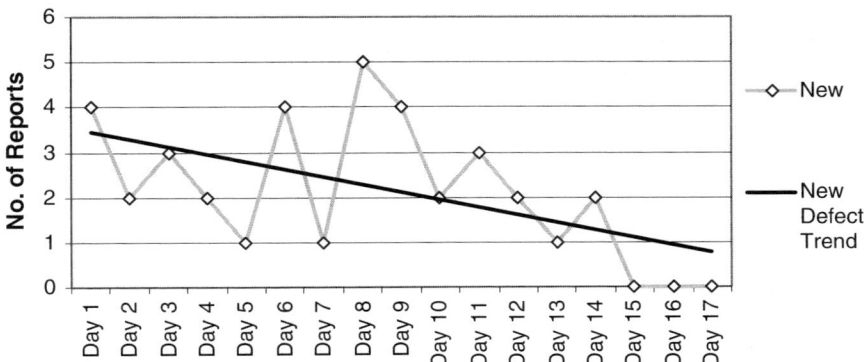

Figure 7-8 ● Recent New Defects

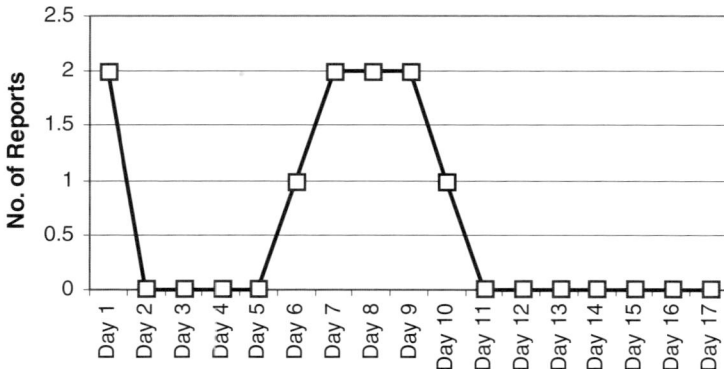

Figure 7-9 ● Bad Fix Rate

Based on this data, the project team has a moderate level of confidence that they will meet their date. The number of defects in the backlog, when analyzed using discovery, closure, and bad fix data, is not as daunting as it first appeared.

● SOME CHEESE WITH THE WHINE

Finger-pointing happens in every organization, usually when the stress is already extremely high and the last thing anyone needs is a litany of unfounded complaints. Confronting the accuser seldom does any good, especially if the confrontation is in a public setting like a staff meeting. Even when you have quantitative data at your disposal, sometimes what appears to be a direct approach really is the wrong approach altogether. Generally, the whining and accusations are symptoms of a process or organizational problem. That's what needs attention, not the whiner.

Here's a sample scenario.

The senior staff meeting was unpleasant to say the least. For the fifth week in a row, everyone listened to the development manager whine about how the development slips are all due to poor requirements work up front. "We never get the requirements nailed down until the last minute." "The requirements are always changing." "If we had decent business analysts, my team could deliver on time."

Everyone knows that the requirements generation process needs work. It would help if there were a travel budget to get the business analysts to the customer sites for some face-to-face reviews and actual signoffs. It would also help if the development team didn't start coding before they had the requirements in hand. Nonetheless, it's time to stop the finger-pointing. You catch up with the requirements manager on the way out.

"Got a moment?"

"Sure."

"Let's go to my office. I have something to show you."

On the way there, you congratulate the requirements manager on her patience. "Thanks," she replies. "It's getting old. Jack's been whining up the management chain for weeks, saying that the project overruns are due to my requirements team. We're by no means perfect, but I'm sure we're not the only problem. I'd like to know what's really going on."

"I can help you with that," you reply.

Back in your office, you bring up the data from last week's defect analysis (Figure 7-10) and show it to the requirements manager.

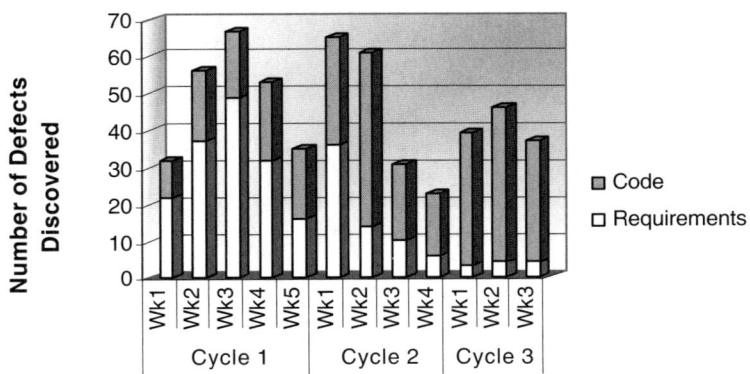

Figure 7-10 ● Defects Rates by Injection Phase, Cycle, and Week for Jack's Products

"What's this?" she asks.

"It's the answer to your question. Based on my last three cycles in development, I'd say Jack's got some explaining to do."

Pointing to the trends on the chart, you continue. "The test team discovered many defects related to requirements in the first cycle, but that number has dropped off since the second cycle. In fact, in the last two cycles, the majority of defects have been due to code mistakes. If there's a problem here, it isn't with your business analysts."

"Can I get a hardcopy of that?"

Click. "On its way. Anything else you need?"

"No, this is great stuff. Thanks."

The requirements manager is almost out your door when you call her back. "Please do me a favor and talk to Jack in private about the code defect rate rather than bring this up in a staff meeting. The coding mistakes are just a symptom of a larger problem that isn't his fault."

"And what's that?"

"The Director insists on double-assigning his resources. Effectively, that means that Jack's cycle times are cut in half. When that happens, his injection rates go up. I'm meeting with the Director this afternoon to try to get that changed."

"OK, but if he starts bashing my team again. . . ."

"I don't think he will. He hasn't seen that data yet."

"I see. So you're making me the bearer of the bad news?" she replies, smiling.

"It has to be *someone*. I'm just a PM, and you know nobody around here listens to PMs . . . ."

● THAT'S MY RESOURCE!

Time measures can be problematic when there is pressure to meet chargeable-hour quotas or to produce more with fewer resources. If your data shows that you have been able to meet dates in spite of blockage and interrupts, that's good news for you and your team. You've learned from the past, planned for the obstacles you knew would come, and performed to that plan. But it's also bad news, because instead of being congratulated for your expert risk management, you can be criticized for not making your direct-charge hour quota, or you can be penalized by being expected to do more with less.

Here's another sample scenario.

You watch as the conference room slowly fills up with tense, tired faces. This is the fourth special staff meeting your VP of Engineering has called in the last month. No one expects the situation has improved since the last meeting.

"As you know, we are running badly in the red this quarter and need to increase revenue." The VP doesn't even stop to look around the room—that's not news to anyone. "Our CFO has just issued the following policy statement: Going forward, all development teams are expected to be 95 percent chargeable to their assigned project. However, overtime required to meet that goal is not to be logged on the timesheets. That will raise our operating costs and defeat the purpose of the increase in chargeable productivity. It goes without saying that all scheduled dates must be met. You can inform your teams that layoffs will be considered at the end of the quarter unless revenue increases. That's all I have. Any questions? No? Good. Have a nice day."

After the boss leaves the room, there's an agitated discussion about how to meet the chargeable-hour requirement. Not only is 95 percent productivity atypical in project management planning, it's also unrealistic in software, where the industry data suggests that productivity is much lower. Then there's the problem of what the "assigned projects" are. The VP is constantly taking resources from one project and putting them on another project to keep his numbers looking good.

As the managers file slowly out to give their teams the news, you return to your office, shut the door, and pull up your spreadsheets. You have six months of task data: direct labor hours, blocked time, and unplanned productive time. It's almost second nature now to plan this extra time into your schedule. You look at the most recent milestone data you shared with your team (Figure 7-11)—lost resources, blockages, and still a 93 percent earned value for the project segment. The team's done well. But you can't take that data in to the CFO, not in that form anyway. You can hear him now: "Excellent. So I can lay off a third of your group tomorrow! Thank you." This will require a bit more "creativity" on your part.

You actually have three issues to address. The first is the 95 percent requirement. That's a function of direct labor hours worked. Second, there's the assumption that only one project is being worked on. That assumption is not only false, but it impacts your ability to meet the direct labor hours requirement. Third, the blockages and lost-resource issues impact your direct labor hours on that "one project."

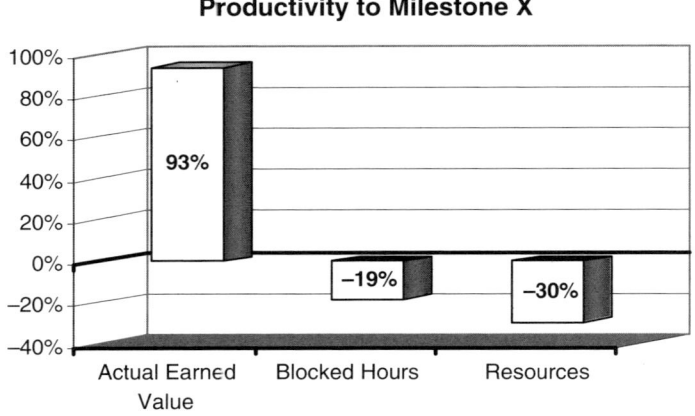

Figure 7-11 ■ What the CFO Shouldn't See

If you can get the CFO to understand that your direct labor has to be spread out across more than one project, that will solve your chargeable-hours problem. On the other hand, you'd also like to be able to show that the blockages and unplanned labor hours are a coordination and prioritization issue that the CFO needs to help solve. You realize that the selling point will have to be current loss of efficiency and longer-term impacts.

So you change the way you look at the data. Instead of looking at how well your team did in spite of the obstacles, you look at what might have been accomplished. If you look at this from the corporate viewpoint, the blocked time is really a conflict of priorities: you needed something from someone who didn't think your need was as pressing as other things they had to do. From the same perspective, the time your resources were working on other projects represented an organization-wide resource management issue: someone else needed your folks at the same time your project manager needed them.

The time lost when you lost 30 percent of your planned resources is about the same amount of time it takes your team to do the system-level requirements for a moderately sized new function, code a moderately sized new function, or fix five defects in the code. You change the labels of the time categories you use for your own tracking purposes and include the time for a design or code effort. The graph tells a good story (see Figure 7-12), and you bring a copy with you to the CFO's office.

"I'm sorry to bother you, but I was hoping you could give me some advice about how best to meet your new guidelines."

"Certainly, come in, sit down."

"The challenge my team faces is how to meet conflicting program schedules. As you can see from this chart, my team loses a significant portion of its chargeable hours to organization-wide issues with scheduling and resource allocation. We . . . ."

He interrupts you. "Stop, please. I don't understand. What are these conflicts?"

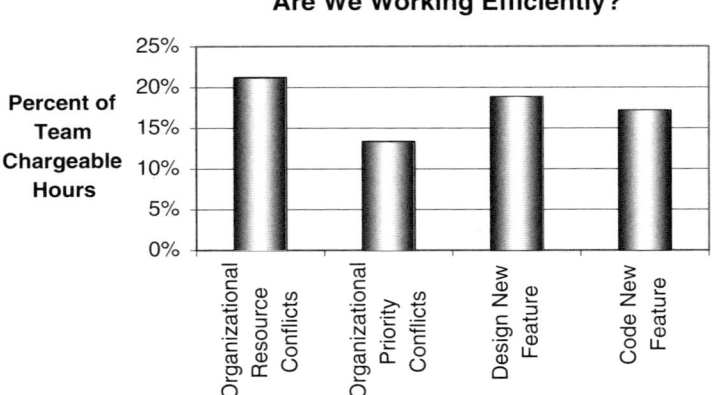

Figure 7-12 ● Resource Allocation Charted for the CFO

You were hoping that would get his attention. "These conflicts arise when different departments or projects have different priorities. For example, there are cases where my resources are pulled off to work other projects even though they are committed to my project." You hope the CFO is getting the impression that your team is in high demand.

"And the 'new feature' columns are what?"

"What we lose when we don't coordinate our work organization-wide. It's not just a question of hours charged one place or another. It's an issue of efficiency and return on investment. In the time I lose to conflicts between projects, I could complete a major piece of design or coding for my current project."

"And why can't you tell the other project manager to wait?"

This is not the time to complain about your VP. Fortunately, you have a better answer prepared. "I can do that. I often have to do that. But that's not in everyone's best interest. Project priority is a business decision; I don't think you want project managers making those decisions on their own."

"No, you are correct, that's not their decision to make. How accurate are these numbers? Is this just a one-time occurrence, or is this loss of productivity a common problem?"

"These percentages have remained fairly constant for the projects that have come through my department in the last year. I can't speak for the other project managers. I don't know what data they collect."

He thinks for a moment. "I assume that when you give a resource to another project, they are completing a deliverable for that project. So this time is not wasted, just allocated elsewhere. Is that correct?"

"Usually. There are, however, cases where even on the new project, my resource is blocked waiting for some other department to complete a task. In the worst case, that can account for about 19 percent of their chargeable time."

"That's much too high."

"I agree. But again, that's an issue of coordination across departments that is well beyond the scope of my developers."

"Well, you asked for my advice, and my advice is that you have your resources charge to whatever project benefits from their effort. I don't want project managers using another project manager's resources for free. They must be held accountable for meeting their approved budgets and not hiding expenses in the time tracking system. This priority problem is disturbing and I will bring it up at the next senior staff meeting. I will get back to you if there's any other information I need. Does this answer your question?"

"It most certainly does. Thank you."

● SIZING UP THE SITUATION

Faced with a new project and a demoralized or unfamiliar project team, you can introduce measurement concepts through an exercise. This is not just an opportunity for team building. It also can help you assess the team's capabilities, although you should corroborate your impressions with others if you can. In this scenario, a defect typology exercise reveals the need to rethink the release plans.

Here's the scenario.

"I came right over when I got your voice mail. What's up?"

"Craig, you've probably heard that I fired Dan this morning. I'm giving you his product."

"What?!? What have I ever done to you? You're kidding, right?"

"No. You're the only PM I have free right now. It's a mess, I know. Last release was 100K in the red, and we got slaughtered in the field. The account managers will have our heads if that happens with this release. Won't be easy, but I'm sure you'll pull it off."

"Thanks a million. And do I get a bonus for being the sacrificial victim?"

"I can guarantee I'll pay you at least until the project is over."

"That's what I like about you. You never overcommit. Guess I'd better get on it."

"Good luck."

It's a lengthy walk to the software development department—long enough for you to start thinking about a fast food restaurant franchise or starting a crime scene cleanup business, but too short for you to come up with a brilliant solution before you get to the development lead's cubicle.

"Hi Jane. I guess I'm your new PM."

"We were hoping you'd replace Dan. Have a seat. What do you need from me?"

"I need to know what really happened with 2.0. I've heard all the rumors but I haven't had a chance to look at Dan's project plan or financials yet."

"Well, let's see, we didn't get the requirements nailed down until late in the cycle, finished coding just three weeks before it shipped, cut the test time by two-thirds. The usual, in other words. Right now there are 200 software problem reports in the queue for the next release."

"How many do you usually have as a backlog?"

"About 20."

"Great!" Flipping burgers is looking better and better. "In 25 words or less, tell me what's wrong with the product."

"It should have been retired years ago, but they keep selling it, promising all sorts of enhancements, and we're left to patch it as best we can."

"Do we have the requirements for 3.0?"

She just looks at you.

"When are they due?"

She's still looking at you.

"OK, OK, I get the idea. Round everyone up and I'll meet you in the war room."

That gives you enough time to excavate Dan's project binder from a mound of printouts, desk toys, and soda cans on what used to be his desk. The hand-drawn timeline indicates he'd scheduled a three-month cycle, all of it devoted to coding except for two weeks of testing at the end. The requirements were due from the regional account managers last week. Coding has already started. The sound of a copier in the distance reminds you of french fries sizzling in the deep fry vats.

The team has assembled in the war room. All eyes are on you.

"Everyone pumped for 3.0?" You get the smirks you expected. "On Dan's plan, we were supposed to have requirements already, and of course you've all started coding up the enhancements." The smirks widen. "Obviously, I need to get the account managers on board with this project before we can worry about release requirements. Right now, I want to talk about product requirements."

"Aren't they the same thing?" asks one of the testers.

"Apparently not, given the defect backlog," you reply. "We have two development streams here: the first is the backlog, the second is the new requirements for 3.0. Assuming that the account managers give us the usual useless stuff, we'll need to interpret it in light of product requirements before we code it up. So, tell me about the backlog."

You hear a few horror stories about customer outages and some grumbling about the politics surrounding this or that problem report. The number 200 keeps coming up. They clearly don't know what you're asking for.

You toss three whiteboard markers to different team members and ask them to list the kinds of problems they think the customers have. One person starts listing the modules that have defects. Another tries listing the issues each customer has. The third team member simply jots down "navigation, pulldowns, printing."

"Thanks, you can all stop now and sit down. The torture is over. Which of these lists can we use to generate product requirements?" There are a few hushed votes for the different lists. "You're all correct. Each of these gives us clues to what the product is supposed to do. The first identifies the code level risks we have where we seem to break things. The second list shows us who pays the price for our mistakes. And the third list highlights the visible effects of those mistakes. In short, where the problem is, who sees it, and what they see."

"Next question: How are you going to address the backlog? What will you work on first?"

You get the typical answers: "Do all the fixes to a single module at once." "Highest priority first." "The ones the account managers yell loudest for."

"Which ones matter most to the customers?" you ask. "Do you have the defects broken down by severity?"

Jane rummages in her notebook and hands you a graph of severity by customer (Figure 7-13).

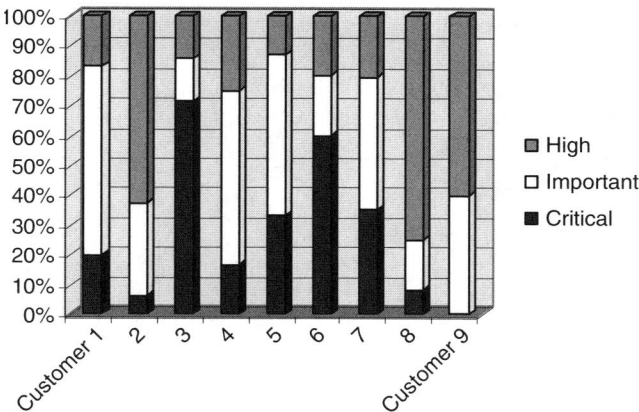

Figure 7-13 ● Percentage of Release 2.0 Defects by Severity and by
Customer

"How much of the backlog is this?" you ask.

"There are 178 reports that are high or above," she replies.

"In that case, severity rating won't help us prioritize the back-log. There are too many defects, and there's little consistency from one customer to the next in the distribution of severities. We need a different tool. I want you to break up into two teams. Team 1 will analyze the list of defects for the who and the what: which custom-ers experienced which kind of failure. You'll have to make up your categories for kinds of failures. Team 2 will analyze the list of defects for the where: what part of the product failed. Team 2 will have to determine how to divide up the product. Try to get through all 178 reports in one hour. Don't worry about not having full definitions for your categories. The point of working through the list under a tight timeline is to have the definitions come out of the defect data itera-tive hypothesis testing, as it's called. Let's meet back here at 2 p.m. and we'll go over your results."

In the afternoon meeting, you're pleased to see that Team 1 caught on right away. They've brought some handouts (Figures 7-14 and 7-15), and you give their spokesperson the floor.

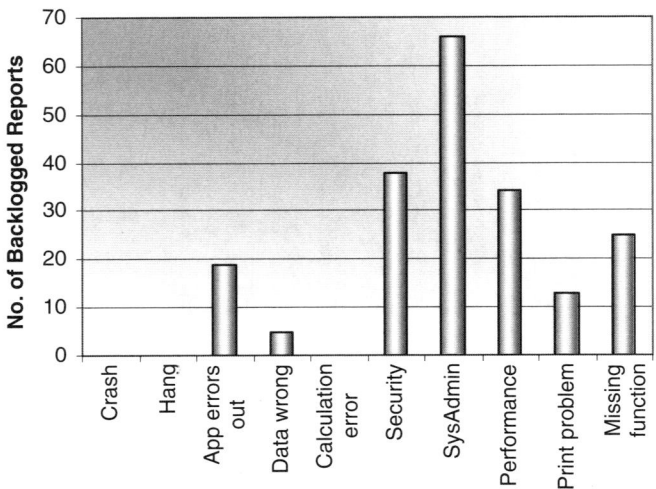

Figure 7-14 ● Analysis of Error Types by Category

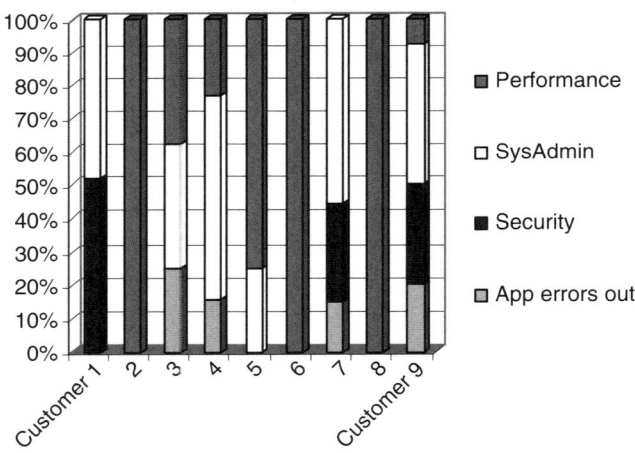

Figure 7-15 ● Relative Percent of Highest Incidence Categories by
            Customer

"When we went through the defect list, we found something interesting. We expected the "critical" and "important" reports to be system crashes and things like that. They weren't. The first graph I passed out shows the categories we used to define what kind of failure the customer saw. Most of the reports involve setup or security issues."

"Then we looked at which customers were affected by which problem category. That's the second graph. We decided to ignore the category of missing function because we assumed that was a problem with the original requirements. We didn't read every problem report in detail, but we saw some trends: the administrative user interface is confusing, some security settings apparently can conflict with one another, and you can lock down parts of the application without knowing it. That's what's behind the application errors and maybe some of the performance problems."

"Excellent work, thank you. Team 2, it's your turn. Where do the problems lie?"

"We had a lot of trouble with this," replies one of the developers. "We couldn't come up with any high-level categories without actually working out the fix itself. On a first pass, though, the bugs seem to be scattered across the whole code base."

"So you're telling me our problems aren't all based in these two components?" you ask.

"Looks that way."

"I don't suppose there's a design spec for the administrative or security functions?" you ask.

"No," Jane replies. "And we didn't touch that code much during the last release. The new work was mostly in transaction logging."

"How did that get tested?"

"We had a pre-acceptance test with a couple of the account managers. That cost us almost a whole week for fixes."

"By the time those fixes were done, we only had a few days to test the rest of the product," adds the test lead.

You nod sympathetically. "Thank you, everyone. We've made good progress toward prioritizing the maintenance work. I need to talk with the account managers a bit before I can give you a detailed schedule. Jane, stay for a minute, please. The rest of you are free to go."

You close the door behind the last of the team members. "I need to put you on the spot, I'm afraid. I don't know these folks very well, haven't worked with any of them before. Let me give you my first impressions and you can correct me if I'm wrong."

"OK."

"First off, based on the response from Team 2, I'll guess the development team as a whole doesn't understand the product, just the code. You probably have mostly career programmers, with no business or user experience."

"Right so far. Same problem with the test team. They have to have requirements or they can't do anything."

"I thought so. How much time does it take you folks to turn around a problem report from the test lab?"

"By the end of version 2.0, we were closing three or four reports a day."

"I'm sorry, what I meant to ask was how long does it take for a report to be closed?"

"You mean from the time we actually start working on it?"

"Yes."

"Oh, anywhere from two days to a week."

"So with, what, eight developers and 178 defects, at two to five days a shot. . . ."

"Want my calculator?" she asks, offering her PDA.

"No thanks, too hard to swallow. I need something with a smaller form factor that's guaranteed fatal. Like cyanide."

"Any other good news I can give you?"

"As a matter of fact, there is. I want you to estimate two things for me. First, how long will it take the team to review all the transaction logging code changes? Second, how long will it take the team to fix and test the issues Team 1 discovered today? I'll need this by tomorrow morning."

"Can do."

"In the meantime, I'm going to suggest to the account managers that we make version 3.0 a maintenance release. There's plenty of work to do in maintenance for the next two and a half months. The account managers are already late getting requirements to us. And there are clearly different product utilization profiles in the customer base. The account managers have to explain to us why some customers see performance problems while others see application failures. If we can guarantee a solid maintenance release that improves customer satisfaction, we can actually use this backlog as the selling point."

Jane nods. You continue. "My real concern is that somewhere along the line we destabilized this product. Defects concentrated in a few areas I can deal with. If they really are scattered everywhere, then we may be looking at systemic design problems without the right resources to handle them. The bottom line is, we can't do a new features release right now." You start for the door. "Time to go talk to the account managers."

"Good luck," she says. Then Jane asks, "Craig, why is your hand twitching?"

"It is? Must be subconsciously practicing for my next career."

"Flipping burgers?"

"How'd you guess?"

"You wouldn't last a day. 'Fast and cheap' just isn't your style."

● KNOW WHEN TO USE PLAN B

There are times when you have no choice but to delay your project. Your reasoning may be based on technical issues, team issues, or both. The trick is to have enough quantitative data to feel confident in your new date.

Consider this scenario.

You've just taken a new job as a project manager for an IT department. Your predecessor left suddenly—more than two months ago—under circumstances that no one is willing to talk to you about. But you've been around the block a few times and you're sure it has something to do with the current release, due to be installed company-wide in two weeks.

The schedule indicates that you have to roll out a new accounting package on the Friday before Christmas, December 21. Since the whole company will be out on holiday the next week, your predecessor clearly was planning to use that week as contingency time in case of minor delays toward the end of the project.

The engineering manager has been running the project for the last two months. He stops in on your first day to tell you that they are working through some last-minute quality problems. He's told the development and test teams they will work weekends, Christmas Eve, and Christmas Day to fix all the defects and then install over the rest of the vacation week. The company will have its application when they return from Christmas break, he says—a bit too confidently. He leaves after inviting you to his defect review at 1:00 p.m.

Knowing there's sometimes a fine line between bravado and flat-out lying, you take a look at the defect tracking system. It's an Access database with no real reporting capabilities, but after 15 minutes of manual work and a spreadsheet, you've got the overall picture. The data is not reassuring (see Figure 7-16).

In the last 15 days, the project has accumulated a substantial backlog of defects. That may be leveling out, but it will take a few more days to determine if the decrease in the backlog from Day 13 is a trend or just a temporary trough. What's also puzzling is the steady increase in the backlog. You expect to see peaks. It stands to reason that there will be days when the number of defects being discovered is higher than the number being fixed. But it also is reasonable to expect that there will be days when the number of fixed defects is high enough to bring the backlog down again. It appears that more is awry here than just the usual end-of-project time crunch.

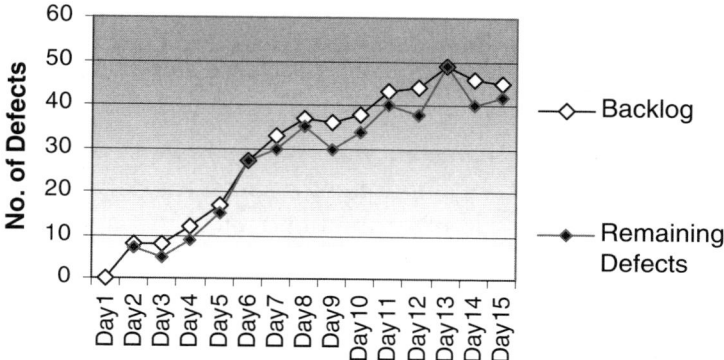

Figure 7-16 ● Defect Backlog

The afternoon defect review is pretty much what you expected. The test lead reads through the list of new and unclosed defect reports, the developers estimate the time to fix them, and the engineering manager reminds them they are running out of time. When the review is over, you call an impromptu status meeting with the development and test team leads.

You ask them how the testing is conducted, what the fix and retest process is, how much time these activities take, and where the inefficiencies are. It takes a while to coax this information out of the leads. They exhibit clear signs of burnout and morale problems, and they're obviously accustomed to having managers challenge anything they say. From the test leads, you learn that only half the testing is completed. The team finds 5 to 10 defects a day. In the last couple of days, the fixes have been rejected by the test team. All the testing is manual, linear, and user-operation based.

When it's their turn, the development leads tell you that their folks can only fix one, sometimes two defects a day. It can take them two days to fix a database or calculation problem. When a defect is found, the developer has to stop what he or she is doing, review the issue, and estimate the time to fix in preparation for the daily defect review. Builds take three hours and are started every evening so the build is ready for the test team to install the next morning.

What kinds of defects are being found? you ask. You hear about boundary condition problems and data integrity issues, pieces missing from the user interface, and errors in some of the calculations. What's the relative ratio to date? About the same, they tell you. When you ask why these problems are there in the first place, you get the usual litany: because there's no interface specification, no design, no time to unit test the code before the build, etc.

That's enough information for an initial diagnosis. "Thank you," you say, standing up and pausing just long enough to get their full attention. You can almost feel them cringe, expecting another "overtime and Christmas" speech. "There's no way this product can be rolled out on time. I will speak to the engineering manager. We'll meet back here at 4:00 p.m."

Back in your office, you start to work out the details. Using the number of defects in the current backlog, the number of developers, and a 66 percent productive time rate, you can determine how long it will take to complete the fixes for the existing backlog. Assuming no change in the defect discovery rate, you can estimate the number of defects discovered over the next two weeks. Is that a *valid* assumption? There's no way to tell without more data than you have at your disposal. But it is a *legitimate*, if pessimistic, assumption.

The linear testing approach has discovered about the same number of various types of defects, and the types include both design and coding errors. There's no reason to believe that the rate will decrease if the current testing approach is maintained. Nor is there any reason to believe that the types of defects discovered will change, so you can't count on finding only simple, quick-to-fix problems in the next two weeks.

Your next stop is the engineering manager's office. You bring with you the charts shown in Figures 7-17 and 7-18.

"We'll have to slip the install date into the New Year," you announce.

"Why?"

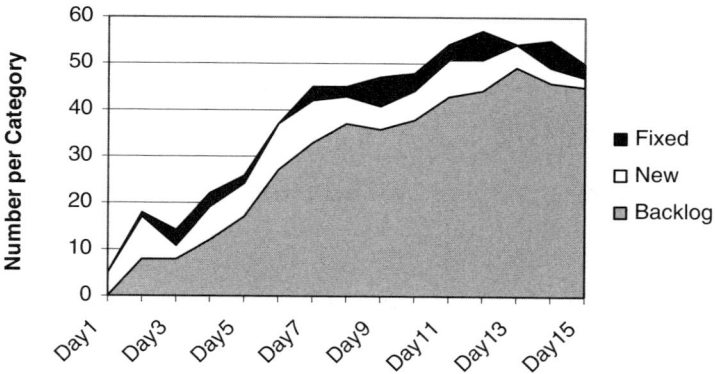

Figure 7-17 ● Fix-cycle Rates

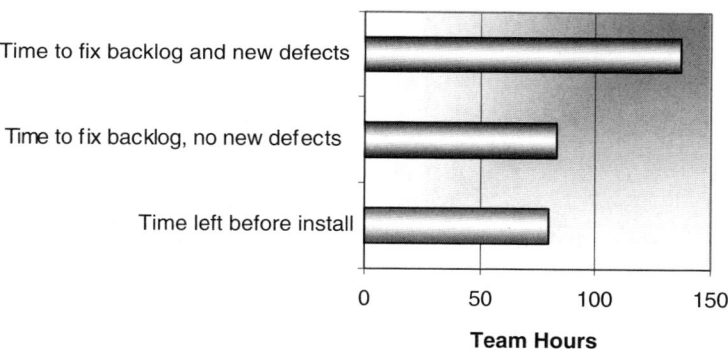

Figure 7-18 ● Projected Time to Complete the Cycle

"This is the current defect profile," you reply, handing him the area chart. "Notice the large area. That's the backlog. The other areas show that the team is finding as many defects as it fixes on a daily basis."

You give him the bar chart. "Based on the time it currently takes to fix and retest defects, it will take more than the time left in the project just to complete fixing the backlog. When I estimate the number of defects we'll find between now and the original installation date, it pushes that installation date out by more than one week. That doesn't include any time for a final acceptance test before rollout."

"Then the team will have to work double shifts."

"That won't get us where we need to be. The recent defect rate includes a high bad-fix rate. That means the developers are making code changes that don't fix the problem. That wastes time for both development and test. If that rate continues, you can double the delay. Making this team work 16-hour days guarantees the rate will at least double, maybe even triple."

"The CIO and the PMO will be very disappointed to hear this," the engineering manager says ominously.

"Disappointment builds character. Tell me, how will they take it when we bring a third of the company to a standstill thanks to a premature installation?"

He is silent for a moment. Then he says, "What do you suggest?"

"Install to a select group of users on January 4, the Friday after the holiday break, then roll out the final product to the rest of the departments the following Friday. We'll call it early user training. After all, it's a very complex product and it's just common sense to roll it out in waves rather than all at once."

"We'll have to meet this new date, you know. No delays, no excuses, no defects. Or else."

"The product will be as good as your initial requirements-gathering work, which I'm sure was thorough and complete. As for the date, we'll install it on the CIO's desktop at 11:00 a.m. Thursday, January 3."

"All right. I'll take the news to my Director. You speak to the PMO."

"No, I'll take care of all that." As you start out the door, you add, "One more thing. I'll take over day-to-day management of this team starting now."

"Fine by me. It's all yours." He looks understandably relieved.

So far, so good. The engineering manager is out of your way and you've succeeded in buying some more time for the team. Was it enough? Will you be able to give the team December 22 through 25 off? You certainly should be able to give them a short break if you get rid of the inefficiencies in the daily operations. Something will have to be done about testers interrupting developers for defect analysis, developers interrupting what they are doing to create estimations for defects they really haven't examined fully, builds that take up developer and tester time but don't really contain enough new fixes to warrant the time, and a serial test approach that's generating defects indiscriminately. Making changes to address these inefficiencies isn't rocket science; it's just a matter of whether the team can absorb several sudden changes.

At 4:00 p.m. you reconvene the development and test leads meeting. Their long faces indicate that they are expecting the worst. "Our new delivery date is January 4. That gives us some time, but we have to use it wisely." You proceed to outline the new policies. Builds will occur Monday and Thursday nights. Defects having to do with calculations, data integrity, interfaces with other applications, and other serious deficiencies in the current backlog will be fixed first. Testers will continue to use their test scripts as written, but they will only report on defects in those areas. When the product has been wrung through the test scripts once and the serious defects have been found and fixed, the process will begin again.

You've been in monologue mode for 10 minutes. No one has said a word. No one's even smiled. Trench syndrome makes for tough audiences.

"These changes are effective immediately. Your goal is to make it through two iterations on this product by close of business on Friday, December 21. That way you'll have only user interface and simple error fixes to worry about when you come back to work from your holiday break on December 26. Merry Christmas." You walk out of the room, wondering how long it will take for what you said to sink in.

● APPLYING WHAT YOU'VE LEARNED

There are no measurement exercises this time around. Assuming that you read the appendices when they were referenced in previous chapters, you have only a few paragraphs to go before this book is finished. When you close this book, you will have a new set of tools and techniques to help you manage your software development projects. If you've worked through the exercises at the end of the other chapters, you will also have a coherent measurement architecture, a rough implementation plan, and some key documentation for starting up your measurement program.

You should also have a greater appreciation for the role the software project manager can play in the organization as an agent of change and, therefore, as a leader. Software development projects are like tiny societies. A group of people within the same business culture follows a shared development "lifestyle," working together toward a common goal, playing different but interdependent roles. This mini-society is seldom self-governing, however, especially in low-maturity organizations. The software project manager must assume many roles—governor, law official, fire fighter, banker, and sometimes even social counselor.

It's a difficult challenge, one made more difficult by the fact that while the software project manager may have ultimate responsibility for the success of the project, he or she does not have complete control over the social and political environment. Neither a despotic nor a laissez-faire management style is appropriate in such situations. The despot pretends to have power and control that he or she really doesn't have over the complexities of software development, while the laissez-faire project manager refuses to exercise what power and control is legitimately and necessarily his or hers to wield.

Somewhere in between these two extremes lies the ideal software project management style. This style shares many of the attributes of good leadership skills: vision and agility, leading by example rather than by decree, and leveraging the potentials within diverse personalities and work styles to create well-coordinated teams. In an industry where the market, the workforce, and the tools are constantly changing, being a good leader often means being an astute change agent as well. The software project manager often must change the existing workflow to suit the project's needs. He or she often must change the way people do their individual tasks if the project's schedule and deliverables are to be met. But you can't mandate productivity, schedule adherence, and quality—you can only nurture the individuals who collectively make these goals a reality.

So now, with your head full of measurement jargon and sample graphs and dozens of application guidelines, it's time to step back and ask yourself what you will do with all this information. By that, I don't mean how you will implement your measurement effort. I'm talking about how you will use measurement in your role as change agent and in your role as leader. Specifically:

→ How can you apply measurement to improve both product and working conditions?

→ What real benefits can be derived from these measures and indicators for you, your project team members, and your company?

These are tough questions. They have many possible answers. Some of the answers might be wrong today but right six months from now. Some answers might be right for some part of your team but not for your organization, and vice versa. It's all very confusing and complex. But if you liked things simple, easy, constant, and certain, you wouldn't be pursuing a career in software project management, would you?

APPENDIX

A

The Rationale for "Mixed-Methods" Measures

Throughout this book, you have encountered instances where conclusions were drawn from a very limited data set. Sometimes, those conclusions also drew from qualitative information, such as other factors that "might" be affecting the data or knowing a bit about the team's history. The guidelines for interpreting measures presented in the book were certainly not statistically valid inferences. So it is quite reasonable to ask whether these (or any such guidelines) have any validity as analytic tools.

The short answer is: It depends on what you mean by validity. Can our common-sense judgments and interpretations be "valid," or is validity only possible in logically or statistically sound claims? Suppose a project manager makes a decision about ship readiness based on her past experiences, on a gut feel. Suppose it turns out that the decision was the right one. Was that a valid decision or was it just a lucky guess?

As long as there are only two options available—mathematically or logically sound decisions and everything else—the question is merely rhetorical. The manager's decision lacked the data and formal reasoning needed to qualify as a valid conclusion. It was subjective and invalid, no better than a lucky guess. But more than two options are available, as the social sciences have learned.

For many years, research in the social sciences had to emulate the paradigm of physics. The empirical or "positivist" approach required researchers to treat their subjects in much the same way as closed-box testers treat software: conclusions were drawn from macro-level behavior treated as a series of inputs and outputs. More recent movements in social scientific research have challenged that paradigm, and they have offered a series of methodological alternatives now referred to as qualitative research methods. Interestingly, many of these approaches are also found in software process improvement.

Taxonomic analysis in social science is similar to the defect classification schemes that can be found scattered across the software process literature. Process flowcharting and root causal analysis in software are similar to the techniques of matrix analysis and event analysis in social science. In the analytic approach known as grounded theory, sociologists categorize observed behavior and generate hypotheses about behavioral patterns, in much the same way as iterative methods or formal reviews are used to "validate" software work products. After all, a software design is not significantly different from a hypothesis about human behavior. Each tries to determine how the subject or function will, or should, work. Each is tested by observation in the field or in the test lab. Each is subject to revision based on input from those tests.

In effect, the qualitative methods that sociologists use in fieldwork are also used in the software industry. The similarity should not be surprising, as the subjects of analysis in the two fields are also very similar. Sociologists study a complex entity comprising people, language, ideas, behavioral patterns, and culture. Process improvement experts study a complex entity comprising people, language (such as requirements), ideas (such as designs), behavioral patterns (such as procedures and code patterns), and culture (such as development lifecycles or project management approaches).

When the sociologist publishes the results of qualitative research, the researcher's conclusions are subjected to scrutiny using a concept of validity quite different from the one used in formal logic and statistics. The research is evaluated for how well it prevented the researcher's biases from skewing the results. The researcher is expected to use triangulation with other subjects and with other researchers to determine if the results are convergent with other similar research. In this case, validity is not obtained by subsuming a behavioral pattern under some theory. Valid conclusions are credible conclusions that provide insight into experience or behavior. More than a lucky guess but less than a theoretical deduction, these conclusions have credibility because they fit all the known facts and because anyone can follow the line of thought that leads to the conclusion.

What is known as the "mixed-methods" approach in social science combines quantitative with qualitative approaches. Qualitative techniques such as one-on-one interviewing or narrative historiography supplement and help illuminate quantitative, objective evidence. The mixed-methods researcher places objective data in its human context, but also triangulates an individual's input with input from others and with the relevant quantitative data. The assumption behind such an approach is that all knowledge has a pragmatic aspect—it has to be useful in solving a problem, improving something, or meeting an emotional need. So it is possible in a mixed-methods approach to see narrative history, subject interview information, and behavioral attribute data mixed together and focused on a proposed solution or change in behavior.

This is also what happens in a "ground up" measurement effort. The software project manager doesn't just start collecting and using quantitative data about the product quality or the team's productivity. The taxonomy, the categories of defects and time, come from the actual experiences of the project team. The matrices for the analysis—"derived measures"—come from a combination of team input, departmental (or cultural) goals, and the availability of objective data to measure. To do an adequate job of time tracking, the project manager has to talk to team members and get their input about time categories and time expenditures to set up the taxonomy. But the manager also has to talk with the individual team members to find out exactly what they were doing in the assigned time. This is the narrative history that turns the quantitative time-per-task data into a qualitative guideline you can use in the next project.

In software metrics programs, software measurement is a tool for determining compliance. In the environments for which this book was written, software measurement is a mixed-methods approach to understanding why software development projects go awry and how to get them back on the right track. In the metrics program, the researchers are observers, looking at control charts and histograms to ensure that all is going as planned. In the measurement effort described here, the researcher is a participant as well as an observer, and the activity is self-reflective and cyclic, more than purely analytical. The difference between statistical process control and a mixed-methods measurement effort reflects a difference in corporate climate and day-to-day needs. Using a mixed-methods approach to help you manage the daily crises in your department doesn't in any way impact the validity of your decisions; it simply changes the criteria.

Some readers may find it sad that I have spent so much time defending the "methodological legitimacy" of what they see as plain common sense. However, I think it is important to position the techniques and interpretive methods used here in the larger context of software quality assurance. The mixed-methods approach to software measurement is as legitimate an approach to solving software development crises as it is to social behavioral research. Moreover, unlike purely quantitative approaches, it escapes the admonition, attributed to Pliny the Elder, that one should not confuse measurement with understanding.

APPENDIX

B

An Alternative Approach to Severity and Priority

In the early 1990s, the storage software engineering team at Digital Equipment Corporation developed a way to analyze and prioritize defect reports. That system and some early results of its application were described in a conference paper in 1995. At the same time, engineers at IBM were developing what has now become known as Orthogonal Defect Classification, which uses a very similar approach. The IBM approach has been described in several publications, and the implementation details have been documented in conference proceedings and on several websites. This appendix is a revised extract from that 1995 paper and describes part of the approach that Digital's storage management software used.[1]

Anyone who has spent time in defect review meetings or has sat on Change Control Boards knows that the traditional status pair of severity and priority is at best contentious and at worst misleading. All software defects are critical problems to *someone*. What's more

---

[1]Kelsey, R. B. "PARSE: Problem Analysis and Process Management for Software Maintenance." *1995 Proceedings.* Pacific Northwest Software Quality Conference (Portland, OR: 27–28 September 1995), 423–433.

important than that final status assignment is the debate that goes on before it.

When a Change Control Board tries to evaluate a defect report and determine its significance, the discussion usually involves two issues:

- How widespread is the problem? That is, how much of the installed base is likely to encounter this defect?
- How often might the defect appear on a site? That is, does the defect appear in typical, everyday operations or is it an unlikely event requiring specific and unusual conditions?

The goal of the storage software team in Digital Equipment Corporation was to standardize and codify the discussion of defect priority and severity. The original system included a series of analysis matrices that covered all facets of the defect and problem report, from the strategic importance of the reporting customer to the bad-fix history of the defective component. Only those matrices used to assign priority and severity will be discussed here.

If we know a problem's frequency of appearance, we can differentiate between a politically sensitive customer complaint and an inexcusable technical blunder. If we know a defect's penetration in the installed base as well as its frequency of appearance, we can address those problem reports with the highest risk to the installed base.

The table in Figure B-1 shows a sample matrix for penetration into the customer base. This matrix is used in the analysis, before the root cause is known, so the matrix uses criteria based on rather coarse differentia—whether the defect affects all customers or exists only in the current release, whether it is hardware- or configuration-dependent, etc. The penetration matrix approaches the defect from the perspective of configuration management and specifies the actual, versus perceived, severity of the problem in terms of customer exposure.

But penetration in the installed base is not sufficient to prioritize the problem report. Configuration dependencies are only half the story. We also need to understand the exposure from an operational

Penetration Characteristic	Priority
Problem possibly affects all current customers	5
Problem probably occurs in a specific release	4
Problem possible only in this base level	3
Problem manifests in a specific software configuration	2
Problem manifests in a specific hardware configuration	1

Figure B-1 ● Penetration Matrix

point of view. This involves two more matrices, frequency and operational dependency.

Frequency in Figure B-2 is not the incidence of the problem report but instead reflects the potential incidence of the defect's symptom(s). Thus, a problem report that is generated during "normal" product functions would have a higher priority than one that requires a specific hardware/software interface for its manifestation. A problem that manifests itself in local system operation is reasonably higher priority than one that occurs in a distributed environment, on the assumption that if the code is defective in local functions, it is likely to be defective in widely distributed functions.

Operational dependence differs from frequency in that it looks at the defect from the perspective of the software architecture and its defect history. The example in Figure B-3 is clearly skewed toward availability and reliability, and assumes a functionally mature user interface. Other situations would call for different characteristics and different priorities, e.g., installation problems, performance issues. In this case, the matrix was created based on our knowledge of the failure modes of our product and the types of defects we introduced. The priority values reflect a mix of criteria, with user-visible fre-

Frequency Characteristics	Priority
No unusual context	5
Specific local event sequence	4
Specific distributed event sequence	3
Specific hardware/software interface	2
Not known/irreproducible	1

Figure B-2 ● Frequency Matrix

Operational Dependence Characteristics	Priority
Normal user-initiated operation	7
Failure of normal user-initiated operation	6
Internal error recovery on a control operation fails	5
Internal error recovery on a data operation fails	4
Distributed synchronization fails	3
System interface call fails	2
Resource initialization	1

Figure B-3 ■ Operational Dependency Matrix

quency at the top, fix complexity and risk in the middle, and typical coding blunders at the bottom.

Considered in conjunction with operational dependence, the product/system effect matrix shown in Figure B-4 helps identify the impact on product availability and reliability. Failure in a system interface call may not be high priority for the product seen in isolation. If that failure results in a system crash, obviously the defect needs to be found and fixed before, say, we investigate an incorrect status display. The priorities of local and distributed operations have been swapped here compared to the frequency matrix on the assumption that a failure in a distributed operation impacts more users than one that occurs locally.

Using the priority values in the matrices rather than a single priority or severity rating allows the development team to assess the impact of the defect *and* the risk of the fix. A problem with high penetration, in a function frequently used, with deleterious effects on the customer environment, obviously needs immediate attention, but it also carries a greater liability if the fix is a "bad fix." Similarly, a fix to a problem in distributed operations that currently results in system

Product/System Effect Characteristics	Priority
Data corruption	6
System failure	5
Distributed operation failure	4
Local operation failure	3
Incorrect status displayed	2
Unacceptable performance	1

Figure B-4 ■ Product/System Effect Matrix

crashes has higher risk potential, and will require more testing time and resources, than will a fix to a performance deficiency that affects only a specific hardware platform.

The purpose behind the typical priority and severity ratings is to help development manage its workload. The matrix approach described here is a better approach because it does away with the subjective aspects of priority and severity assignments, and inserts a risk assessment based on technical criteria into the typical "find, fix, retest" cycle.

Further Reading

● **CLASSICS, MODELS, AND APPLICATIONS**

Bridge, N., and C. Miller. "Orthogonal Defect Classification Using Defect Data to Improve Software Development." *Proceedings of the Seventh International Conference on Software Quality* (Montgomery AL: 6–7 October 1997), 197–213.

Chrissis, M. B., M. Konrad, and S. Shrum. *CMMI®: Guidelines for Process Integration and Product Improvement* (NY: Addison-Wesley, 2003).

Evans, M. W., and J. J. Marciniak. *Software Quality Assurance and Management* (NY: John Wiley & Sons, 1987).

Fenton, N. E. *Software Metrics: A Rigorous Approach* (NY: Chapman & Hall, 1991).

Gilb, T. *Software Metrics* (Cambridge: Winthrop Publishers, 1997).

Grady, R. *Practical Software Metrics for Project Management and Process Improvement* (Englewood Cliffs, NJ: Prentice-Hall, 1992).

Grady, R., and D. Caswell. *Software Metrics* (NY: Prentice-Hall, 1987).

Humphrey, W. S. *A Discipline for Software Engineering.* (NY: Addison-Wesley, 1995).

Humphrey, W. S. *Managing the Software Process* (NY: Addison-Wesley, 1989).

IBM Center for Software Engineering. Papers available on Orthogonal Defect Classification at http://www.research.ibm.com/softeng/.

IEEE 1061-1998. *IEEE Standard for a Software Quality Metrics Methodology* (NY: IEEE, 1998).

ISO 10006:2003. *Quality management systems – Guidelines for quality management in projects* (Geneva, Switzerland: ISO, 2003).

ISO/IEC 15939:2002. *Software engineering – Software measurement process* (Geneva, Switzerland: ISO/IEC, 2002).

Jones, C. *Assessment and Control of Software Risks* (NY: Prentice-Hall, 1994).

Kan, S. H. *Metrics and Models in Software Quality Engineering* (Reading, MA: Addison-Wesley, 1995).

Kelsey, R. B. "Integrating a Defect Typology with Containment Metrics." *Software Engineering Notes,* 22.2 (1997), 64–67.

Kelsey, R. B. "PARSE: Problem Analysis and Process Management for Software Maintenance." *1995 Proceedings.* Pacific Northwest Software Quality Conference (Portland, OR: 27–28 September 1995), 423–433.

Kruchten, P. *The Rational Unified Process: An Introduction* (NY: Addison-Wesley, 2004).

Mair, S. "A Balanced Scorecard for a Small Software Group." *IEEE Software* (Nov./Dec. 2002), 21–27.

Möller, K. H., and D. J. Paulish. *Software Metrics* (London: Chapman & Hall, 1993).

Niessink, F., and H. Van Vliet. "Measurements Should Generate Value, Rather than Data." *Sixth IEEE International Symposium on Software Metrics* (1999), 31–39.

Paulk, M. C., et al. Software Engineering Institute. *The Capability Maturity Model: Guidelines for Improving the Software Process* (NY: Addison-Wesley, 1995).

Phillips, J. J., T. W. Bothell, and G. L. Snead. *The Project Management Scorecard* (NY: Butterworth-Heinemann, 2002).

Poulin, J. S. *Measuring Software Reuse* (NY: Addison-Wesley, 1997).

Pressman, R. S. *Software Engineering: A Practitioner's Approach*, 4th ed. (NY: McGraw-Hill, 1997).

Pulford, K., A. Kuntzmann-Combelles, and S. Shirlaw. *A Quantitative Approach to Software Management* (NY: Addison-Wesley, 1996).

Putnam, L. H., and W. Myers. *Five Core Metrics: The Intelligence behind Successful Software Management* (NY: Dorset House, 2003).

Rico, D. F. *ROI of Software Process Improvement: Metrics for Project Managers and Software Engineers* (Fort Lauderdale, FL: J. Ross Publishing, 2004).

Royce, W. *Software Project Management: A Unified Framework* (NY: Addison-Wesley, 1998).

Schulmeyer, G. G. "Software Quality Assurance Metrics." *Handbook of Software Quality Assurance*. Edited by G. G. Schulmeyer & J. I. McManus (NY: Van Nostrand Reinhold, 1997), 318–342.

Weller, E. F. 2000. "Practical Applications of Statistical Process Control." *IEEE Software* (May/June 2000), 48–55.

● GRAPHING GUIDELINES AND INTERPRETATION

Burnette, R. E. *Technical Communication*, 3rd ed. (Belmont, CA: Wadsworth Publishing Co., 1994).

Coe, Marlana. *Human Factors for Technical Communicators* (NY: John Wiley, 1996).

Craig, M. *Thinking Visually: Business Applications of 14 Core Diagrams* (NY: Continuum, 2000).

Tufte, E. R. *The Visual Display of Quantitative Information* (Cheshire, CT: Graphics Press, 1983).

● MIXED-METHODS APPROACHES

Creswell, J. W. *Research Design: Qualitative, Quantitative, and Mixed Methods Approaches* (Thousand Oaks, CA: Sage Publications, 2003).

Lincoln, Y. S., and E. G. Guba. "Paradigmatic Controversies, Contradictions, and Emerging Confluences." *Handbook of Qualitative Research*, 2nd ed. Edited by N. K. Denzin & Y. S. Lincoln (Thousand Oaks, CA: Sage Publications, 2000), 163–188.

Marshall, C., and G. B. Rossman. *Designing Qualitative Research* (Newbury Park, CA: Sage Publications, 1989).

Schwandt, T. A. "Three Epistemological Stances for Qualitative Inquiry." *Handbook of Qualitative Research*, 2nd ed. Edited by N. K. Denzin and Y. S. Lincoln (Thousand Oaks, CA: Sage Publications, 2000), 189–213.

● SOCIAL-COMPLEX NATURE OF PROJECTS AND TEAMS

Agar, M. "We Have Met the Other and We're All Nonlinear: Ethnography as a Nonlinear Dynamic System." *Complexity*, 10.2 (2004), 16–24.

Bardyn, J., and D. Fitzgerald. "Chaos Theory and Project Management." *Proceedings of ProjectWorld 97*. Vol. 1. (Washington, DC: ProjectWorld Inc., 1997), E4/1–12.

Harvey, D. L., and M. Reed. "Social Science as the Study of Complex Systems." *Chaos Theory in the Social Sciences*. Edited by L. D. Kiel and E. Elliot (Ann Arbor: Univ. of Michigan Press, 1997), 293–323.

Haslett, T., and C. Osborne. "Local Rules: Emergence on Organizational Landscapes." *Nonlinear Dynamics, Psychology, and Life Sciences*, 7.1 (2003), 87–98.

Kelsey, R. B. *Chaos and Complexity in Software: Challenging the Industry and the New Science* (Commack, NY: Nova Science Publishers, 1999).

Lumley, T. "Complexity and the 'Learning Organization.'" *Complexity*, 2.5 (1997), 14–22.

Robertson, R. "Chaos Theory and the Relationship between Psychology and Science." *Chaos Theory in Psychology and the Life Sciences*. Edited by R. Robertson and A. Combs (Mahwah, NJ: Lawrence Erlbaum Publishers, 1995), 3–15.

Young, T. R. "Chaos Theory and Social Dynamics: Foundations of Postmodern Social Science." *Chaos Theory in Psychology and the Life Sciences*. Edited by R. Robertson and A. Combs (Mahwah, NJ: Lawrence Erlbaum Publishers, 1995), 217–233.

Index

204